TOXIC POSITIVITY

HOW TO BE YOURSELF, AVOID POSITIVE THINKING TRAPS, MASTER DIFFICULT SITUATIONS, CONTROL NEGATIVE EMOTIONS AND THOUGHTS

CHASE HILL

Copyright © 2021 by Chase Hill

All rights reserved.

The content contained within this book may not be reproduced, duplicated or transmitted without direct written permission from the author or the publisher.

Under no circumstances will any blame or legal responsibility be held against the publisher, or author, for any damages, reparation, or monetary loss due to the information contained within this book. Either directly or indirectly.

Legal Notice:

This book is copyright protected. This book is only for personal use. You cannot amend, distribute, sell, use, quote or paraphrase any part, or the content within this book, without the consent of the author or publisher.

Disclaimer Notice:

Please note the information contained within this document is for educational and entertainment purposes only. All effort has been executed to present accurate, up to date, and reliable, complete information. No warranties of any kind are declared or implied. Readers acknowledge that the author is not engaging in the rendering of legal, financial, medical or professional advice. The content within this book has been derived from various sources. Please consult a licensed professional before attempting any techniques outlined in this book.

By reading this document, the reader agrees that under no circumstances is the author responsible for any losses, direct or indirect, which are incurred as a result of the use of information contained within this document, including, but not limited to, — errors, omissions, or inaccuracies.

CONTENTS

A Free Gift to Our Readers   5
Introduction   7

Chapter 1: The Culture of Oppressive Positivity   13
Chapter 2: The Dangerous Effects of Toxic Positivity   25
Chapter 3: How to Recognize and Avoid Toxic Positivity Traps   37
Chapter 4: Nine Powerful Techniques for Healthy Thinking   63
Chapter 5: How to Master Your Emotions   91
Chapter 6: It's Ok not to be Ok — Simple tricks to cope with your negative emotions   108
Chapter 7: How to Control Your Thoughts for Optimistic Outcomes   130
Chapter 8: Getting Through Those Challenging Experiences with a Little Less Misery   145
Chapter 9: How to Deal with Toxic Positivity from Others   160
Conclusion   169

Your Free Ebook   189
Resources   191

A FREE GIFT TO OUR READERS

29 WAYS TO OVERCOME NEGATIVE THOUGHTS

I'd like to give you a gift as a way of saying thanks for your purchase!

* * *

In 29 Ways to Overcome Negative Thoughts, you'll discover:

- 10 Strategies to Reduce Negativity in Your Life
- 7 Steps to Quickly Stop Negative Thoughts
- 12 Powerful Tips to Beat Negative Thinking

To receive your Free Ebook, visit the link:

free.chasehillbooks.com

Alternatively, you can scan the QR-code below:

If you have any difficulty downloading the ebook, contact me at chase@chasehillbooks.com, and I'll send you a copy as soon as possible.

INTRODUCTION

Most of us love a good oxymoron. Expressions like the *living dead* and an *estimated guess* shouldn't make any sense, but they do. One of the newer implausible combinations of words is toxic positivity. If you're living, you aren't dead. So if something is positive, how can it be toxic?

The ultimate goal for anyone who has ever suffered from negative thought patterns will be to become a positive person. The world is full of positive people and positive messages that should inspire us towards this optimistic mindset. We have memes and positivity gurus, friends who let nothing affect them. That's the goal.

The point of an oxymoron is often to emphasize a conflict. It makes us think about the complexity of a term. Positivity isn't toxic, but toxic positivity is an extreme that some people use to force the negative thoughts away.

Toxic positivity is a nasty trap. It looks bright and shiny, polished a little more by today's pop culture. Rather than accepting our wide range of emotions and learning how to deal with them, we pin a smile to our faces and say everything is perfect.

On the other hand, there will be people in our lives who promote toxic positivity. For example, if you are having a bad day, a partner or friend may quote an unrealistic movie line rather than listen to your feelings.

They won't even realize what they are doing most of the time. But unfortunately, people feel like this type of advice is helpful. It's certainly easier than actually getting their hands dirty with some real feelings. "Think happy thoughts" puts an end to the problem, or so people assume.

Toxic positivity is addictive. Whether it's your own mind or someone else's advice, we say things like "Hakuna Matata" and start singing along to the song *No Worries* from the Lion King. And for that moment, we feel better.

The next time we have negative thoughts and emotions, we start singing the same happy tune. We put up a false barrier and block the negative vibes. I am not the only one who used to think they were living in a positivity bubble.

We must learn how to find the balance between the two extremes!

We can't live our lives with the heavy weight of negativity on our shoulders. But we can't avoid our real feelings and go to the other extreme of toxic positivity. By reading this book, you will learn techniques that will allow you to understand what you are feeling and to control negative thoughts and emotions rather than pushing them to one side.

We will start this journey by understanding toxic positivity and the toxic positivity trap. We will then work on the full range of emotions so that each experience is dealt with in a way that brings about the best outcomes.

Life is meant to give us some challenges and obstacles to overcome. But, on the other hand, it provides us with the chance to improve our skills and grow. Instead of looking at these challenges as negatives or covering them up with toxic positivity, we will learn how to process all of our emotions in a healthy way.

It has taken me over a decade to master this balance. In my twenties, negative thinking controlled my life. So much so that I lost everything, including my job, my girlfriend but, more than this, I lost the sense of who I was.

I felt weak, lacked confidence, and blamed myself for not doing something about the spiraling intrusive thoughts. There were numerous articles and TED talks about the power of positive thinking. But, unfortunately, people made it look so easy, as if all I had to do was tell myself that to be positive and find the bright side of each situation.

As you can imagine, this pop-psychology advice comes from people who are confident enough to stand on stage in front of hundreds of people. But, unfortunately, it's not the same for someone who barely had the self-esteem to get out of bed.

After six weeks of trying, my situation was worse. The negative thinking was no better; in fact, my inner voice told me I was stupid for even trying. I started drinking, put on weight, and saw no future for myself. When a friend said that life could be worse, I became angry with this toxic positivity.

A single internet search into "why do people say life could be worse" began my research into different mindsets and negative thinking. Delving into human psychology enabled me to understand how the brain worked. I began to spot the strategies that made sense, and I tried a lot that didn't.

When I started to see a difference in my own life, I decided to help others. I dedicated my time to more learning and research until I was able to give up a job that had no meaning and become a certified life coach and social interaction specialist. Thanks to this change, I have seen a difference in the lives of hundreds of people, each with their own unique set of struggles.

You may not have access to professional help or have

tried strategies that haven't worked. For this reason, I chose to write a series of books related to thought patterns and emotions. Listening to what my clients and readers say, I felt we needed to get to the bottom of toxic positivity and learn its dangers so that more people could find their way out of the trap.

It's perfectly normal for you to doubt your ability to change. However, one point that I always highlight is that any change in our mental attitude takes time. So you won't be forced out of your comfort zone but rather will deal with changes gradually.

With that in mind, the first place to start is understanding what toxic positivity is.

CHAPTER 1: THE CULTURE OF OPPRESSIVE POSITIVITY

If you have never heard the term toxic positivity, you aren't alone. That's not to say that you haven't experienced it. At this point, it is worth mentioning that you may have also been guilty of it. But don't torture yourself over this. Toxic positivity has been drilled into society, and we can all probably think of a moment when we have done the same.

First, let's look at some examples of toxic positivity to understand this complex concept.

Sammi had finished her university degree but found it impossible to get a job because she had dedicated her time studying and had no work experience. As a result, she was getting passed over for jobs in fast-food restaurants by eighteen-year-olds. Initially, she remained positive, eagerly attending interviews, but every no was a knock to her confidence.

Her mom told her that studying would be worth it in the end. But her friends told her that jobs were like buses, you wait for ages and none come, then five come at once. Eighteen months later, Sammi was facing eviction, and the thought of having to move back home was humiliating. But, "Tomorrow is a new day of opportunities," her mom would say.

Jason had the worst experience a parent could have when his son was diagnosed with cancer. The fight was long and hard, and it broke him in every way to watch his son go through this. Like many parents in this situation, he turned to internet forums for advice and support. He received comments like "Keep smiling" and "You're an amazing dad."

Sammi had dedicated four years of her life to the degree that should have gotten her a job in her field. Instead, after eighteen months of rejection, she had every right to feel angry and frustrated. But she couldn't because she was told that she would never get a job with that attitude.

Jason used all his energy and strength to be upbeat for his son. He didn't want to smile, and he didn't need the reassurance that he was a good dad. Instead, he needed to express his grief; he needed to know that it was ok to feel scared and traumatized.

In our darkest times, we need support from those around us. We need someone to listen and just be there for us.

Neither Sammi nor Jason derived comfort from the meaningless advice they were given. Even though no harm was intended, they felt like bad people for having negative emotions, making them feel worse.

Defining toxic positivity

Toxic positivity stresses the need for optimism regardless of how bad a situation is. We regard negative emotions as a weakness, suppressing negative thoughts and sentiments and maintaining positive thinking. Positivity is great, but not when it denies or minimizes genuine emotions.

Imagine your emotions are a form of exercise. Of course, you know that sitting on the couch all day isn't good for you. But, at the same time, extreme exercise can also have its downside.

When people force you to exercise, it doesn't magically make you more active. Instead, it can make you feel worse or even guilty about your inactive lifestyle.

Humans have an incredible spectrum of emotions, none of which is superior to any other. Each emotion has its place and a reason for being there. For example, our fight or flight response kicks in when we are scared—this is essential for survival. When we are angry, it might be because someone has hurt us.

Think about the last twenty-four or forty-eight hours. How many times has someone asked you how you are?

How many times have you replied, "Great" or "Fine thanks" when you feel awful inside? This is toxic positivity. You don't want to say how you really are because it goes against the positive energy we should give off.

What are the signs of toxic positivity?

There are many forms of toxic positivity; toxic positivity could originate from within or from external sources. Here are some of the most common everyday indications of toxic positivity:

- You mask your feelings or try to hide them from others

- You dismiss your own feelings and adopt a "just do it" attitude

- You feel guilty about the emotions you feel, good and bad

- You lack empathy, use a positive quote rather than listening to other people

- You put things into perspective while suppressing the pain you or someone else is suffering

- You reprimand someone for their negative emotions, calling them a "neg-head" or something similar

- Others shame you for your negative feelings

- You ignore problems

- You repeat "feel-good" quotes when faced with a challenge

To further appreciate the extent of toxic positivity in our lives today, let's take a look at some typical comments:

- Just stay/be positive
- Look on the bright side
- It could be worse
- Everything happens for a reason
- Happiness is your choice
- Good things come to those who wait
- Think happy thoughts
- You will get over it
- Never give up
- No point crying over spilled milk
- Don't be so negative
- Don't worry, be happy
- Keep your head up

We have heard these sentences so often that it's hard to imagine how they can harm you. However, these words can be incredibly damaging. If happiness is a choice, it implies that we choose to feel sad and depressed. While it's good to be determined, if we take the attitude never to give up, we risk wasting time on solutions that may at no time be effective. Giving up doesn't mean abandoning the goal—it means finding a more effective way to achieve it.

The dangers of toxic positivity

The next chapter will look at how toxic positivity can be dangerous. But, for now, it's essential to understand the White Bear Syndrome or ironic process theory. When we mask our negative emotions with positive vibes, we are essentially telling ourselves not to think about them. However, trying not to think about something makes us think about it even more.

The White Bear Syndrome comes from an experiment carried out by the founding father of thought suppression, Daniel Wegner, PhD. First, one group of participants was asked to verbalize their thoughts for five minutes while not thinking about a white bear. Then, another group was asked to do the same but think about a white bear. The result showed that the group asked not to think of the bear did so more frequently (Wegner, 1987).

It's a simple experiment you can do yourself to show how true this is. Imagine your absolute favorite food, now don't let yourself think about it for the next five minutes, and carry on reading. Then, write an X on a piece of paper every time this food pops into your mind. Telling yourself not to think about your favorite food doesn't make the image disappear.

Dr Jamie Zuckerman, a clinical psychologist, explains that the suppression of negative emotions caused by toxic positivity can increase levels of anxiety and depression. This will be covered in more depth in Chapter 2.

How toxic positivity is growing

Think back to the 1980s. There were few TV channels and no internet. People would sit down to watch the news at a specific time because 24-hour news channels didn't exist and, of course, people read newspapers. As a result, people didn't have the same exposure to negativity.

The internet gave us instant access to what was going on in the world. But it still required us to search for the news stories we wanted to hear. Then along came social media. These sites were ideal for keeping in touch with friends and family and sharing photos and videos. But it wasn't long before negative images started appearing on our pages.

Toxic positivity has changed the way we post on social media sites too. In the early days, people could post that they were going through a rough time, and there would be messages of support—"call if you need a chat" or "here if you need me."

Now, "trollers" are out to leave hurtful messages and

shame others for their posts. We fear posting how we feel in case we get online abuse. So instead, we only post the positive.

Carrera Kurnik, culture director at Fashion Snoops, explains that the "flex culture" we see on social media sites is a trend whereby people try to show their lives in the best possible light. But, unfortunately, this is only fueling toxic positivity.

For example, perfect family pictures are filtered and photo-shopped. Others look at these unrealistic images and feel worse about their own lives. But the actual harm is being done to those uploading these false posts. They are just hiding behind images instead of looking for ways to improve their lives.

The "positive vibe" people of the world started to overcompensate for the negativity in the world and online, and we are flooded with comments to make us think and feel more positively.

When we see these messages, we fall victim to the same thought. "Yes, it's true. But, I should keep my head up, and I can choose to think happy thoughts." But, unfortunately, this does not change the fact that our lives and the world are filled with pain.

The pandemic has seen a significant increase in toxic positivity. It's probably the first global issue we have touched on since toxic positivity was first understood. Nearly five million people have died from COVID-19 to date. Why on earth should we be positive? That's five million families who have lost a loved one. Some families have lost many people. Others have lost their jobs and homes; they have more debt than ever before. There are restrictions on when we can go out, if we can go out, how we work, and so much more.

Even now, the world is still living in great uncertainty. The virus might appear to be under control, but it's not over. Those who can't travel may not have seen family members in almost two years. When they do get to travel, there will be new fears regarding safety. Others who suffered from mild social anxiety may now feel terrified to leave the house.

Then, some believe the virus is a hoax and refuse to follow CDC guidelines. Videos of people coughing over others on purpose or even licking food in supermarkets have gone viral. It's disgusting and infuriating.

Yet, we are plagued with images telling us to be positive. There is enough bad in the world without adding our feelings of sadness, fear, and anger. Even if you haven't lost someone personally, it is normal to feel sad when nearly five million people have died. It isn't going to make me feel less miserable when someone tells me, "at least it wasn't anyone in your family." If I ignore my sadness, I can't empathize with those who have lost someone.

I confess, the pandemic was a real test of my emotional

state, even after years of understanding my feelings. I often watched the news in disbelief. I questioned what the future would look like. Sometimes, I even had moments when I brooded over my own health. We are only human, after all.

I didn't underestimate the power of these emotions or try to sweep them under the rug. As with the white bear, I knew these feelings would only come back more frequently, even stronger than before.

Was there a bright side to COVID-19? Yes, pollution was significantly reduced during lockdowns. Many of us had time just to slow down and take a moment to reassess our lives. Communities gathered together, and we gained a greater appreciation for key workers who went out of their way for those who were helpless.

We have heard stories like that of Captain Tom Moore, who, at 99, wanted to walk laps around his garden to raise £1,000 for the National Health Service. In the end, he raided over £12 million (more than $16.5 million). These stories are examples of hope and inspiration even during these challenging times.

But it is essential not to look at the pandemic with rose-colored glasses. It still doesn't mean that our negative feelings aren't justified!

On the contrary, we must listen to our negative emotions more than ever. As mentioned before, these thoughts and feelings are often there for our survival. If we suppress the idea that we aren't scared of catching COVID-19, we could become careless, stop wearing masks, stop social distancing and stop washing our hands correctly.

For most of us, this is the first time we have experienced such a deadly pandemic. Nobody really knows how to act in such a situation. That is why it has been so common to see meaningless messages about being positive. So again, don't feel bad if this has or still does apply to you.

When thinking about what toxic positivity means to you and how it impacts your life, the key thing to remember is that positivity is not toxic or harmful. I know that for myself and many others, without the positive stories we have heard during COVID-19, our experiences would have been far worse. Instead, they gave us some hope.

We should be aiming to increase the positivity in our lives and find more joy. We will learn how to do this. But at the same time, we have to understand that negative thoughts and emotions do exist.

To find the perfect balance, we must recognize these emotions and learn how to manage them. It will be like sticking a positivity plaster on a negative broken leg if we don't. We won't solve anything.

Toxic positivity is the extreme of negative thinking. You have likely understood and experienced the danger of negative thinking. After all, the research on negative thinking has been going on for a long time.

When we ignore our emotions, we suffer more, and the consequences can be dreadful. In the next chapter, we will cover why toxic positivity can be detrimental to our health and relationships. It is also necessary to understand why toxic positivity is harming society.

CHAPTER 2: THE DANGEROUS EFFECTS OF TOXIC POSITIVITY

We touched on the concept of toxic positivity in Chapter 1 and mentioned theories like intrusive thoughts and excessive reflection. This chapter discusses what happens when we replace genuine feelings with false optimism.

Firstly, we looked at the white bear syndrome, which states that the more we suppress specific thoughts, the more we think about them.

Secondly, we looked at suppressed emotions, which are those we push back down and refuse to acknowledge. But we can never suppress our feelings because they have a way of slipping out.

One of the favorite analogies I discovered during my research concerned suppressed emotions and energy. Don't worry, not positive energy! Everything has energy, but the energy isn't always balanced. A natural way to create this necessary balance is to release the extra power.

Imagine your negative emotions as energy—subduing is just going to cause it to be released in a different way. Anger is a good example. If your boss criticizes you unfairly, you may suppress this anger, but you will still be angry later on and will take it out on your team. This is called displacement.

The anger could also be displaced onto your parents, partner, or children.

We suppress our negative emotions because we don't want to seem unlikable to others. Nobody wants to be the "Eeyore" in the room. The irony is that suppressed feelings make us less likable to those closest to us because we aren't as happy as we could be.

There is a difference between suppressed and repressed issues, and both are dangerous. Suppressing our emotions is a voluntary act. Thoughts may provoke specific feelings which we may choose to ignore. Repressing our feelings is an unconscious action.

The International Journal of Psychotherapy Practice and Research (2019) listed various studies that illustrate the dangers of repressing emotions:

- People who suppress their feelings are more likely to become ill because they are suppressing their immune system (Pennebaker et al., 1997)

- Continual repression of emotions in the workplace leads to stress, an increase in heart rate, and anxiety. There is also less commitment to the job and, therefore, a decrease in productivity (Cote, 2005).

- One study showed that 84 percent of visits to physicians for common complaints like dizziness and headaches had no medical diagnosis, meaning there were socio-emotional challenges (Kronke, Mangelsdorff, 1989).

- People who struggle to regulate their emotions are more likely to suffer from substance abuse, irregular sleep, poor nutrition, and disordered eating (Lanyon, Almer, 2002).

Nikki was one of the many moms who had a relatively organized life between her full-time job and three children. But, when the pandemic hit, restrictions were put in place and, all of a sudden, there were five people in the house—twenty-four hours a day. Cooking and cleaning doubled; she had to help the children with school work and adjust to remote work.

The first few days were quite novel, and everyone seemed to enjoy this break from routine. Unfortunately, the kids started bickering on day four. Nikki's husband felt the pressure of his own job and wasn't much help. Because of the additional responsibilities, she stayed up later and got up earlier.

Gender aside, this is a perfectly relatable scenario, and Nikki did what the rest of us did. She counted her blessings—her family was fine and had work, there was food on the table. She told herself that it was only temporary and that everything would be fine if she got on with it and stayed strong.

Exhaustion set in. Nikki became irritable with her family. This made her feel guilty because her family wasn't to blame. So she started spending more time alone in her room with the excuse that she was working. This way, these nuisance emotions wouldn't show. She ignored the shortness of breath she was experiencing and the moments of light-headedness.

It wasn't until she had to go to the hospital with chest pains that ER doctors told her she had suffered a mild heart attack—shocking for a relatively healthy woman in her mid-forties.

The danger of trends and toxic positivity

Technically speaking, yoga and meditation are not trends. They have been around for thousands of years and have brought peace and understanding to countless people. Much like the internet and social media, used in the right way, both yoga and meditation can positively impact our physical and mental health. We will discuss these benefits later on.

These ancient spiritual practices have reentered the world with a modern twist. It is now accepted that positive thinking can lead to positive outcomes. However, this is not necessarily helpful.

The danger comes with inexperienced or unqualified instructors who think that yoga and meditation consist of repeating positive affirmations to inspire people to live in this moment of joy and enlightenment. We are not saying that positive affirmations don't work. On the contrary, I have used many and know they do work.

However, the toxic positivity trend of going to a yoga class, having your instructor tell you to breathe and chant "I love myself for who I am" or "The best is yet to come" does not work. These instructors can't tell you to love yourself if you aren't happy with who you are. And they certainly can't promise that better times are to come.

This is the placebo effect. The classroom environment sucks you in, and you believe it to be true. However, as soon as the real world stresses and strains hit, the negative thoughts and emotions re-surface.

Other trends have liberated people and allowed them to talk openly about their feelings. For example, hashtags and social movements enable us to speak freely about global issues such as climate change, equal rights, and immigration.

Thanks to social media, we have seen some courageous doctors and nurses break down and express their true emotions during the pandemic. They inspire us for their work and for showing us that it is OK not to be always positive or falsely optimistic.

Trends can be dangerous because they come and go

rather quickly. People are drawn to popular activities and aren't aware of the potential dangers. Can a yoga class help mental health? Yes. Is it going to make you a positive person who sees results? Not without additional work.

Toxic positivity's negative influence on mental health

There are five significant ways in which toxic positivity can harm your mental health. The first relates to suppressing your feelings. I am a massive fan of understanding how the brain works to understand mental health issues.

1. The negative jar build-up

Suppressing and repressing emotions feed the negative thinking loop. The amygdala (alarm center) and the prefrontal cortex (controlling logical behavior) work together in a typical brain. Any threat perceived by the amygdala, real or not, breaks the connection between the two.

Once the threat is gone, this connection doesn't simply return to normal. The amygdala keeps sending warning messages, but you can't react logically. MRI scans have shown that people who acknowledge their emotions have more significant activity between the amygdala and the prefrontal cortex than those who suppress their feelings (Ellard et al., 2017).

If you continue to receive warning messages but can't logically analyze them and validate them, you will start to experience more significant stress, anxiety, and depression. Emotions that are bottled up become more harmful and more difficult to overcome.

Example: If you lose a loved one, you need time to grieve and process how you feel. You don't need someone telling you that the person who died is in a better place.

2. Friendships aren't real

Friends and social relationships are necessary to bring more happiness into your life. It's not to say that you need dozens of friends to be happy. But a handful of close friends can provide a strong support system and increase your sense of belonging.

Generally speaking, there are two kinds of friends. If you have a friend who is there for you no matter what and can be completely honest with you, you have a bad-weather friend. This is something that sounds bad but is actually very good. This type of friend is dependable, come rain or shine.

Fair-weather friends are those who are there for you when times are good, but as soon as a real problem or a difficult situation arises, they are gone. They are there for the good times but will run away at the first sign of a storm.

Example: You have been trying to have a baby for what

feels like an eternity. A bad-weather friend will listen to your frustrations and fears. A fair-weather friend will tell you it's not your time.

3. Toxic positivity messes with how your brain should react

You're upset. Your brain acts accordingly. When you fake a smile or start saying that everything is alright, your brain gets mixed signals. It can't cope with this—and neither can your body.

People who read your body language are going to be just as confused. We have all seen toothpaste adverts where the model has a huge false smile. We can spot a fake smile by the extremely high eyebrows. When our body language sends mixed signals, people don't know how to react, and we could be missing out on some valuable support.

Example: You didn't get the promotion you had your heart set on. You are doing everything it takes not to get angry or emotional. Your hands are shaking, but you have a grin from ear to ear. Your colleague can see that you aren't happy, but your fake positivity gives the impression that you don't want to talk about it, further suppressing your emotions.

4. Toxic positivity makes you sadder

We judge ourselves for how we feel in certain situations, specifically in social situations. When we think others expect us not to think negatively, it makes us sadder (Bastian et al., 2012). It's a case of feeling bad about not being positive.

Example: You are at a party, and your body language isn't sending the happiest signals. Someone asks you what is wrong, and you reply with "Nothing, I'm having the best time." You feel bad because, really, you just want to go home, but you feel you should be enjoying yourself.

5. There is a dark side to false happiness

Empathy is the ability to understand others' emotions. Having a permanent bright outlook on life promotes the idea that everything is wonderful in the world. This can lead people to see others' pain as meaningless or non-existent.

It's possible we only see the bigger positive picture and not the small details that give us the whole story. This has been observed in a study of ten- to eleven-year-olds. Happy and sad children were asked to find an embedded object. Happy children took longer to find the object than sadder children (Schnall et al., 2008). This difference in cognitive abilities could be explained by happy people seeing the bigger picture.

Example: At a family gathering, you are exuding positivity—everything is just perfect. It is impossible to imagine that your cousin has challenges they are working through because everything is so great. You are minimizing or invalidating their feelings.

Put it into practice

Now that you are more aware of what toxic positivity is, think about how it affects your life. Are there certain people that push the notion of toxic positivity? Or can you think back to when you were the one who gave the toxic advice?

When you have thought about toxic positivity and your mental health, consider the potential dangers to society as a whole. Can you relate to these problems?

How society suffers because of toxic positivity

We have already touched on the pain of losing a loved one. Whether it's COVID-19 related or not, there are stages of grief that people need to work through. This might take a few weeks or months. There is no set time for this. Rushing or skipping a stage could make the process longer. When we hear advice like "It's time to move on with your own life", you are being pressured into moving through the grieving process.

Social movements, like #MeToo, have allowed people to speak out about abuse. Society has made progress. But toxic positivity can quickly undo this progress. In 2020, there were twenty-nine studies on domestic violence and positivity bias.

These studies showed that being overly optimistic might encourage those in an abusive relationship to underestimate the signs (Sinclair et al., 2020). Should you forgive and forget a partner who is verbally or physically abusive? Looking on the bright side of situations like this can encourage people to stay with their abusive partners.

All relationships require communication, and more importantly, honest communication. If we have to hide our emotional state from those we love, the relationship isn't built on trust. We tell people close to us that we have had a great day hoping that we don't infect them with our negativity. But really, it's just a lie.

All of the above could lead to a sense of isolation. So rather than facing the world with a false smile and some positive quotes to get you through a situation, it's just easier and safer to stay at home.

For many, the pressure to appear happy in the face of adversity may make them feel isolated and ashamed of their feelings. They may feel a stigma attached to their feelings of loneliness and depression. As a result, the American Psychiatric Association estimates that half the people who have a mental illness don't receive the necessary help (n.d.).

Despite its misleading name, toxic positivity may be harmful, leading to severe consequences for our health. While there are techniques to help, some people might be struggling with more than one mental health issue and may need professional help. There is no shame in this.

No part of this chapter is meant to scare you. As toxic positivity is still a new field, many people can't imagine the harm of a false positive phrase. It's even more difficult for someone battling negative thoughts and ashamed that they aren't just happier.

If you find it hard to see how toxic positivity affects your life, the following will reveal certain traps that are very easy to fall into.

CHAPTER 3: HOW TO RECOGNIZE AND AVOID TOXIC POSITIVITY TRAPS

Chapter 1 uncovered some of the most common toxic positivity traps or signs. This crucial chapter will examine these traps and use constructive strategies to deal with them.

The nine traps of toxic positivity

Trap #1: You mask your feelings or try to hide them from others

Sometimes we fear other people's reactions to our emotions, which is why we hide them. We might be nervous about people dismissing how we feel, or we might worry about them getting angry or feeling sad. As hard as it seems, you must remember that you are only responsible for your own emotions. So if you feel upset about the way somebody is treating you, you have to think about your own health, and it is essential to express your feelings.

It helps when you express your emotions in a way that keeps the focus on your feelings rather than the other person's behavior. For this, we use "I" statements.

Look at the difference between "You make me mad when you disrespect me in front of our friends" and "I feel mad when you disrespect me in front of our friends." It's a slight difference, but the listener doesn't feel as if they are being attacked.

When it is time to start opening up more about your feelings, begin with those you trust the most. Even if you aren't ready to confront people who stir up negative emotions, it will still help you talk to a friend who actively listens.

Put it into practice

If you haven't already done so, I highly recommend starting a journal. Research into Major Depressive Disorder (MDD) showed that expressive writing for twenty minutes, three days in a row, significantly reduced depressive symptoms (Krpan et al., 2013).

There is no right or wrong time to write in your journal. Often, it will depend on whether you are a morning or evening person. You might reach for a pen and paper when your emotions are running high or when you want to write about a recent experience. Here are some tips that will help you when journaling:

1. Choose the right journal for you. Don't assume that it

has to be pen and paper. Many people today choose to keep a digital journal.

2. Always start with the date. This will help you remember what you were going through when you look back.

3. Be completely honest. We often imagine people reading our journals in years to come, but that causes us to censor our writing and goes against the whole idea.

4. Try to add as many details as possible. Think of all of your senses, the sounds, and smells, be specific about how the food tasted or the location's atmosphere.

5. Include your emotions, and again, be specific. Then, from your feelings, work backwards until you find the source or cause of that emotion.

Keep your journal handy and create a routine whereby you write every day. Know that this is an entirely safe place where nobody will judge you. This is a great place to stop masking your feelings and become more aware of and comfortable with your emotions.

Trap #2: You dismiss your own feelings and adopt a "just do it" attitude

Ignoring how we feel is a form of negative self-talk known as self-invalidation. When we go through a particular experience, we tell ourselves that our emotions are not justified. The most common trap comprises phrases starting with should and shouldn't.

For example, "I shouldn't feel stressed about my job when my colleague has it worse" or "I'm just stuck in a rut, and I should just get on with it." It's not enough to tell yourself your emotions are valid, even if this is true.

Try to see if there are any patterns to your self-invalidation. For example, are there circumstances or people that seem to encourage you to suppress your feelings? What is making you feel this way?

Next, think about the specific language you are using. We often invalidate our feelings because we are covering up something that could be more painful to deal with. For example, if you ignore your feeling of stress, ask yourself why you are stressed. Is it because of too many responsibilities, or did you make a mistake at work and feel ashamed?

Finally, you have to learn how to be more compassionate towards yourself. Feeling bad doesn't make you a bad person. And although you feel bad, the feeling itself isn't bad until you ignore it.

Put it into practice

Whether you want to start validating your emotions when talking to others or in your journal, get good at explaining why you feel the way you do. For example, instead of saying things like "It's nothing, I'm just tired", be specific. For example, say, "I'm tired because I have an important meeting next week and I'm losing sleep."

Trap #3: You feel guilty about the emotions you feel, good and bad

Social media is the trap here. We read other people's positive posts and feel bad about our own negative thoughts. If we have a moment of positivity, we feel guilty because of other people's problems. Even though our logical brain knows these posts might not be true, it's hard to avoid the trap.

Social media distancing or even a detox can give your mind a chance to break free from this trap.

Put it into practice

There are different ways to limit your social media. First, try switching off notifications. This way, you won't open the page with every new ping. Set aside five minutes in the morning and five minutes in the evening to catch up. Be very strict with yourself, or you will end up spending longer.

Choose the amount of time you want to spend on a social media detox, perhaps a weekend or an entire week. Commit to this time. If you are typically quite active, you might want to create a post to let others know you are digitally detoxing. Don't forget to have other planned activities to fill the time you would generally be on social media.

You may also want to go back to wearing a wristwatch. If the only way you check the time is with your phone, you will be tempted to see what is happening in the digital world.

Social media likes and follows trigger a release of dopamine in the brain. Dopamine is associated with reward behavior. An overdose of social media causes the brain's reward system to release dopamine when really, no reward has been earned, unlike when you reach a goal or master a new skill. Detox from social media gives your brain a chance to reset dopamine levels.

Trap #4: You lack empathy and, rather than listening to other people, you use a "good vibes" quote

This is entirely subconscious. If it weren't, you would be a narcissist, and we know you aren't because narcissists wouldn't read this book—they don't see they have a problem! You aren't a bad person who gives out lazy advice. It's what y feel the other person needs to hear.

Before a toxic positive phrase slips from your mouth, ask yourself if the person you are talking to has asked for your advice or opinion. If they haven't, they need you to simply listen. Learning how to listen will help develop your empathy skills.

Put it into practice

The next time you see someone struggling, ask them if everything is OK. Then, create a test to enhance your listening skills. Two hours after the conversation, you need to write down the three main things your friend said in detail. Getting better at listening will help you provide valuable advice when asked.

Trap #5: You put things into perspective while suppressing the pain you or someone else is suffering

Putting things into perspective enables us to understand the actual situation or value of something. This is a good thing because it often provides us with more clarity. For example, if you have a fight with your sibling, putting it into perspective would be understanding the significance of what you said.

But the downside to putting things into perspective is that we often compare our situation with that of others. And this leads to the "It could be worse" syndrome. A client, Jan, told me about a house she was trying to buy. There was problem after problem, delays with paperwork, problems with evaluators, and then COVID-19 hit. Even after things started opening up again, there was a surprise tax bill for thousands of dollars. It took an exhausting three years to buy the house.

The whole time she told herself and everyone else that it could be worse. Putting her situation into perspective meant comparing what she was going through with someone who was homeless or someone who couldn't afford a mortgage.

It didn't take into account that Jan had been working

seven days a week to save for the down payment. That her partner hadn't helped with the paperwork or that the sellers were getting more nervous by the day.

Yes, it could be worse, but suppressing and not validating what Jan was feeling wasn't fair on her.

Put things into perspective by analyzing situations and not letting problems seem bigger than they are, but don't minimize problems. And don't compare where you are in life with others.

Put it into practice

When you feel you are about to say "It could be worse" regarding your situation, go back to validating the feelings you are trying to suppress. In Jan's case, she was incredibly anxious that there was no end to the obstacles. It is ok to feel anxious.

Saying it could be worse is almost as automatic as breathing. So if you are looking for a way to be stricter with yourself but still kind, start an "it could be worse jar". Stick $5 in it every time you say it and tell others that they have to do the same. One consequence will be that soon you will retrain your brain to stop saying it.

Trap #6: You reprimand others for their negative emotions, calling them a "neg-head" or something similar

We have covered this briefly. Often, we aren't aware that we criticize people for their negative emotions. Perhaps, we feel that people need some tough love to realize that life isn't that bad.

I feel it's important to mention at this point that, now and then, we will come across people who are negative for the sake of being negative. They like the attention. These negative vampires suck the energy out of you, more so when it is just a battle to get through the day.

If someone in your life is particularly negative, it is worth creating some distance until you feel more confident to handle their emotions. That's not to say that you are going to bury this situation. Instead, it's a case of hitting the pause button. Then, when you have the right balance between extremes, you will handle the negative vampires.

On the other hand, many people in your life will go through a rough patch, much like you. And like you, they deserve a chance to express their genuine emotions without feeling bad about it.

When dealing with other people's negativity, remember that they probably aren't blaming you. Don't take their problems to heart. By actively listening and asking the right questions, you will get to the bottom of their emotions. If they ask for your advice, give it to them based on your gleaned information.

Put it into practice

When dealing with other people's negativity, you must have boundaries. Boundaries are your limits based on your values and beliefs, but they are also about your limitations, as the name suggests.

To avoid toxic positivity, we need to promote an understanding that it's ok to express how you feel. So the first step is to allow those around you to say how they feel by listening and not offering unwanted advice.

Boundaries will help you and those around you to understand when their negativity crosses a limit. For example, a friend constantly complains about their partner. First, you listen. Next, you offer advice when they ask for it. Finally, if they don't take your advice and continue to complain about the same problems, you need to set a boundary to protect yourself and, essentially, help them.

Imagine in this same situation—your friend keeps complaining about their partner who smokes. You have listened, they asked you what to do, but they continued complaining. Of course, there will be alternative solutions to the problem, but it's time to set a boundary when you have exhausted your advice.

Maybe your friend didn't take your advice and is still negative. A simple "I love you, but please don't ask for my advice, not take it, and then complain" is enough for them to recognize their own behavior. This is a boundary!

If they take your advice and still complain, it might be that the situation requires professional help. But, on the other hand, they also might be stuck in society's positivity bubble and feel that the problem doesn't warrant it.

Imagine the difference you could make by encouraging medical intervention and getting results compared with telling them that things will sort themselves out. In addition, your relationship will benefit from honesty.

Trap #7: Others shame you for your negative feelings

There are two issues with other people shaming you for your negative emotions. Firstly, you are further encouraged to bury your feelings. Secondly, being shamed causes a person to feel humiliated, shocked, or angry. And it leads to reflection about the type of person you are.

At this point, you are aware that your feelings are perfectly justified. Don't respond immediately because in that moment of shame, your brain is frozen in shock, and you might not be in the best frame of mind to respond. There are people in this world that shame us to get a reaction. Others are unaware of their behavior.

Once you have gathered your thoughts and feel more composed, explain how you feel, again, using I statements. For example, "I feel humiliated when you criticize my emotions." Remember that even if you made a mistake or did something stupid, you don't need to be shamed about how you feel about this.

Put it into practice

Next time someone shames you for the way you feel, drop your jaw in absolute shock. Don't worry about exaggerating this action. Some people won't pick up on a subtle shocked face.

Seeing your face should be enough to let them know that they have overstepped the mark, and your reaction will let them know you are horrified by their behavior without you having to say anything.

This gives you a few seconds to decide whether you want to explain how you feel or get out of the situation. If you can't control your emotions, it's best to let the person know that you aren't willing to talk to them right now, but you will discuss their treatment towards you later.

Trap #8: Ignoring problems

Toxic positivity is a classic avoidance technique. Our finances are the perfect example. At some point in our lives, most of us have lived through hard times when our income didn't match our outgoings. Many are going through this now.

When we fall into the trap of ignoring this problem, we tell ourselves that everything will be fine. But, without intervention, things won't be okay. You will fall behind on payments and end up paying more in interest. You don't need to solve your problems instantly but rather develop a plan.

Put it into practice

It's time to brainstorm. First, we are going to work through a "brain dump." Take a piece of paper and write down all your problems, even if they feel trivial. A successful dump aims to clear the mind of all problems.

Next, organize this list into priorities, most urgent first. You will probably find that some of your more minor problems will be resolved when you resolve the larger ones. So there is a sense of relief to see there aren't as many problems to deal with.

Starting with the most urgent problem, look at different ways to resolve the issues. For example, if it's your finances, you might need a loan, get a second job, or start selling things to increase cash flow. Work through the pros and cons of each to decide on the best option. Then draw up a step-by-step plan to resolve the problem. Repeat for the rest of the list.

Trap #9: Repeating positive affirmations when faced with a challenge

It's hard to stop the long-term habit of repeating positive affirmations. The kids are running around the house screaming, the dog is chasing them, and just as you are about to put the lasagna in the oven, you drop it.

Are you going to say something like, "Don't Worry, Be Happy?"

In the next section, we will look at replacements for the

toxic positivity phrases you use. Right now, you need to come up with a new term to replace all of your go-to positive phrases when times are hard.

Put it into practice

Find a phrase that is neither positive nor negative but puts a smile on your face. More often than not, these are lines from our favorite songs. Here are some ideas:

- Stop, in the name of love (good for taking a pause and a breath)

- I will do anything for love, but I just won't do that (I won't go to the extremes, I won't say yes, when I want to say no, etc.)

- We will, we will, rock you (it's motivating)

- We can be heroes, just for one day (we aren't expecting miracles)

- So what, I'm still a rock star (empowering)

Don't look for hidden meanings in your new phrases. Just make sure that they don't replace your stress, fear, or sadness with positivity.

It's going to take a little time and patience to remind yourself that your feelings are valid and that you shouldn't push them down or replace them with false positivity. Unfortunately, society will still be pushing messages of toxic positivity. The great news is that now you won't be sucked into the same traps as before.

How to replace toxic positive affirmations

Expressing positive vibes all the time is easier than dealing with the real issues at heart, but it is hard to know what to say instead of our typical cheerful phrases.

So, going back to the examples in Chapter 1, we gave you some ideas on how to replace the terms you may have been using.

If someone habitually uses these phrases with you, you can explain why these alternatives are better.

Look on the bright side—I'm here for you, whatever you need.

It could be worse—That's awful. I'm sorry that you have had to/are going through that.

Everything happens for a reason—Sometimes, life can be frustrating. What can I do to support you?

Happiness is your choice—Choose to be your real self and express all of your emotions.

Good things come to those who wait—What can I do to help you achieve your goals?

Think happy thoughts—I will be here for you, good or bad.

You will get over it—You are a strong person going through a hard time. With time, you will come out on the other side.

Never give up—Perhaps it's not that you need to give up but rethink your strategy.

No point crying over spilled milk—That is a difficult situation to be in. How can I help?

Don't be so negative—It's alright if you don't feel positive all the time

Don't worry, be happy—I get the feeling you are worried about something. Do you want to talk about it?

Keep your head up—You can talk to me about your problems; I am here to listen.

It's helpful to remind ourselves and others that pain is part of the human experience.

Nobody can get through their entire life without some form of suffering. With pain and suffering come negative emotions that are hard to deal with.

Having negative emotions doesn't make you less positive. It makes you complete. Imagine yourself as two halves, one positive and one negative.

If you only live your life through one half of yourself, you will miss out on the experiences and growth that can be achieved from the other half.

When you can live life accepting these two halves, you get to appreciate your emotions, relationships, and experiences to a whole new level.

Toxic positivity. Putting the brakes on our goals

Another part of human nature is to have goals—dream of things we wish to achieve, places we want to visit, or even things we want to buy. Some are small, others are larger and require more planning. But it's these things that motivate us in life and essentially add to our happiness.

Goals require work, planning, and effort. Without this, they are simply wishes. Toxic positivity creates desires, not goals.

Emma has wanted her own horse for as long as she can remember. However, her career and children seemed an adequate excuse not to pursue her dream. Instead, she would tell herself to be happy with what she had and that there was a good reason for not having a horse at this time.

For a decade, she told herself that good things come to those who wait. It was as if not chasing her dream now would lead to a better horse in the future. But then something else would come up, and she would feed herself more toxic positivity, like "At least I have my children."

It's true—we can't always have what we want immediately. Ten years ago, Emma wasn't in a good financial situation. But listening to her own toxic positivity created inaction and a lack of enthusiasm towards her goal.

Good things don't come to those who wait; it comes to those who actively work towards their goals. The grass isn't greener on the other side. The grass is greener where you water it.

If Emma hadn't listened to toxic positivity, she would have created a realistic plan to achieve her goal, no matter how long it took. This could have included setting up a separate bank account, looking at land and locations to keep her horse, taking some classes to be better prepared. Each step of her plan would have motivated her towards the end goal.

"Don't Worry, Be Happy" is a very catchy song. Still, it puts us in denial and stops us from taking the necessary action to either get out of a difficult situation or find ourselves in a better one.

Having goals is a unique tool that promotes healthy thinking. In the next chapter, we will go over setting goals the right way to ensure they are realistic. Of course, chasing unrealistic goals doesn't mean you shouldn't think big, but it does mean that your goals should be attainable.

Empathy and compassion can undo the harmful impact of toxic positivity

How many offices have you been in where toxic positivity posters are plastered across the walls? If you are the boss, you might be having one of those "Oh, that's me" moments. But, again, don't be too hard on yourself. It's a trend that many fall for.

We spend a massive amount of time in the workplace where morning meetings, high fives, and the 'just do it' attitude is part of the culture. The idea of showing our true feelings is a sign of weakness. Saying no to additional work or hours isn't going to look good. All the while, we ignore our emotions and any tension to bring a positive vibe to the office.

Stress and negativity in the workplace impact the environment, culture, employee turnover, and productivity. On the other hand, there is a lot of research highlighting the benefits of empathy and compassion:

• A survey involving 1,137 full-time employees in different roles showed the link between workplace distress and a sense of contribution to society. Those people with a greater sense of bonding at work felt they contributed more (Ozaki et al., 2012).

• Compassionate colleagues enable employees to better manage workplace stress and burnout (Figely, 1995).

• A few minutes of interaction with colleagues can steady blood pressure and heart rate (Heaphy and Dutton, 2008).

• Compassion leads employees to feel more valued and cared for. This encourages a more positive attitude towards their tasks and voluntary support for others (Fowler and Christakis, 2010).

Amazingly, it was Florence Nightingale who first introduced empathy and compassion in the workplace. Yet, despite it being in the 1860s, it's only today that companies are starting to adopt these same values in their workplace environments.

Facebook has a flextime program that allows employees to choose when their workday begins and ends, allowing them to work around other responsibilities. Microsoft Garage is a program where employees from any department can get together and brainstorm ideas, even bringing these ideas to life. Prudential Financial provides adult care for employees looking after loved ones at home.

These companies may have more resources than the average company to promote empathy and compassion. However, there are things that you can do as an employee or employer.

As an employee, you can:

● Show more self-compassion as this will encourage others to follow your example. Stop beating yourself up for things you didn't do or could have done better. Instead, learn for the next time.

● Improve your communication skills. As well as

expressing yourself calmly and clearly, become good at listening without interrupting or judging.

• Compassion and kindness require body language as well as words. When appropriate, a hand on someone's arm or a hug can offer much-needed support.

• Cheer your colleagues on and encourage them when they need it. For example, if someone has an important presentation, offer to listen to it so they can practice.

• Take advantage of breaks and the coffee room to get to know people better. Show interest in their lives without bombarding them with questions and coming across as nosey.

As an employer, you can:

Show your compassion

Foster an environment in which you care about your employees' well-being. Offer free water and fruit. Be as flexible with working hours as possible and offer remote work options. In a 2021 global report, sixty-five percent of U.S. employees ranked flexibility as more important than compensation.

Rearrange the office

Traditional desks and cubicles aren't designed to encourage communication between workers. It also enables a sedentary work style where employees sit down for too long.

Productivity increased by forty-five percent when a group of call center employees were offered a chance to work at standing desks (Neurofocus Physiotherapy & Sports Injury Clinic, n.d.). Employees may also suffer from less back pain and burn more calories.

Try to take advantage of areas in the office where employees can walk or stand instead of being stuck at their desks.

Provide times for employees to share their emotions

There are often occasions for various meetings throughout the week, but all will have a strict schedule. Try to organize events, lunches, or a weekly catch-up where employees are given time to talk about their feelings.

In these sessions, rather than asking how a project is going, ask them how they feel about it. Make sure they know that this is time dedicated to talking about emotions and not clients and deadlines.

For example, if an employee says they are anxious about a deadline, the objective isn't to change it. Instead, it's to find out how the anxiety affects them and what can be done to ease this pressure.

Consider encouraging employees to report deaths

Nobody should feel obliged to report the death of a loved

one. However, some leaders, like John Chambers, the CEO of CISCO, ask employees to inform him of any deaths. Leaders and other employees can show compassion or offer compassionate leave.

Introduce a respect-all-ideas policy

Many employees have some fantastic ideas but do not have the confidence to share them. They may fear having their idea ridiculed. Even if their opinion doesn't work out, create a workplace that welcomes initiative, respect, and cooperation. You also get to take in different perspectives, improving your problem-solving ability.

Create an in-house forum

It's hard for people to open up about their emotions, particularly in the workplace. Creating a forum with strict non-judgmental rules gives employees who aren't ready to talk in person a place to express how they feel. You might need to motivate leaders to get on the forum first.

Remember, regardless of your role, the most important thing is to validate people's emotions in the workplace. The result will be an office where people can be themselves—and this will show.

Toxic positivity and our children

If you think of the damaging effects of toxic positivity on other adults, you can only imagine what this will do to children—covering up how you feel sets an example for children.

When parents are blindly optimistic, they might praise their children for everything they do. However, ignoring the negative and overemphasizing only the positive teaches children that anxiety is not normal. Negative emotions may then only be associated with failure (Children's National, n.d.).

Parents naturally want to protect their children from bad things. So, when they have a bad day, they don't come home and tell their children about it. Instead, they will put on the fake happy smile and say everything is great.

While there has to be a level of age-appropriate communication, parents still have to be honest. For example, there is nothing wrong with saying, "I'm a little angry because I got a flat tire, and that made me home late." Then, the next time your child is angry, they will be more inclined to talk to you about it, and together, you can come up with solutions.

There is another side to toxic positivity parenting that we see as perfectly normal, probably because it was the way our parents raised us. So now, with your new understanding, think about these situations:

- Your child is scared of the dark. You have to check under the bed, in the closets, etc. Everything is fine, but your child is still too scared to go to sleep. You say,

"There is nothing to be scared of. Think about some happy things, and you will fall asleep."

• Your child has fallen over, and their knees are bleeding. They are crying. You say, "It's just a scratch; there is no need to cry."

Just because they are children doesn't mean their emotions are invalid. If you want your children to grow up to be emotionally balanced teenagers and adults, you can't encourage them to suppress their feelings at this stage of life.

What's the difference between hopeful optimism and forced optimism?

Forced optimism is the same as toxic positivity. It's denying the chance to feel negative emotions instead of looking only at the positive. Hopeful optimism is when we look at future situations and anticipate the best outcome. This sense of hopefulness can help us to overcome obstacles.

At the same time, hopeful optimism has room for real emotions. It doesn't discount the hardships we go through. For example, you know you have a long day ahead of you, there is probably too much on your list, but you have a list of priorities and are hopeful it will be a successful day—it will be a hard day, but you are hopefully optimistic.

Forcing optimism would be facing the same day and

saying, "What will be will be" or "My positivity will get me through it."

To learn how to put an optimistic spin on some of the challenges we face in life in general, we need to master how to think in a healthy way. That means overcoming negative thought patterns while at the same time not rejecting any negative emotions we may have. It may sound too good to be true, but this is what we will learn in the next chapter.

CHAPTER 4: NINE POWERFUL TECHNIQUES FOR HEALTHY THINKING

It's worth highlighting the name of this chapter. It's not about being a positive thinker. Of course, you will start to think more positively, but if we focus too much on positive thinking, we may overlook the importance of healthy thinking.

For healthy thinking, we need to accept that how we look at situations will influence the outcome. Therefore, we need to appreciate the positives and negatives of a situation. Rather than feeling overwhelmed by the potential negative emotions and results, we should focus on doing what is necessary to improve the situation.

Each of us has emotional and psychological power. When this power is dominated by negativity, we freeze, panic, and become anxious. And this prevents us from moving forward.

On the other hand, when we use our emotional and

psychological power in a healthy way, we analyze a situation, plan effectively, and then opt for an optimistic stance. Healthy thinking isn't ignoring problems and danger. It's recognizing these elements and choosing not to let them control our decision-making.

Why do we feel like mixed emotions are destructive?

Today, even the idea of mixed emotions has negative implications. When you say you have mixed feelings about something, it can imply that you aren't decisive, that you can't make your mind up about whether to feel positive or negative about something.

This has led many scientists and psychologists to ask if happiness and sadness are mutually exclusive emotions. We tend to see these emotions much like hot and cold. You can be one or the other, but you can't be both.

However, if you experience a mix of positive and negative emotions, it just means you can't decide how you feel. While this question has been asked for decades, recent research shows that mixed emotions are not a bad thing; in fact, they can be good for you

Social psychologist, Jeff Larsen, leads the research on the challenging topic. His theory is that instead of seeing things in black and white or negative and positive, there is a third option that involves a mix of both.

This has nothing to do with changing our minds about

how we feel. Instead, it's that certain situations will bring about mixed feelings. Larsen and his colleagues collected experimental evidence to discover the prevalence of mixed emotions.

One example concerned a group of people who watched the movie *Life Is Beautiful*. This comedy-drama follows a Jewish family living in northern Italy when Nazi Germany occupied it. The movie showed some of the horrors that Jewish people experienced, but a young boy's father used humor to protect his child.

Before watching the movie, only ten percent of people reported having mixed feelings. Afterwards, this figure rose to forty-four percent. If you have ever seen this movie, you can understand how it is possible to feel more than one emotion about a particular event.

Another study looked at forty-seven adults who were undergoing psychotherapy. They completed measures of psychological well-being while journaling their thoughts and experiences. In addition, trained raters analyzed their writings for emotional content. The results showed that experiencing happiness and sadness simultaneously led to improvements in psychological well-being (Adler and Hershfield, 2012).

Surprisingly, culture plays a significant role in the ability to experience mixed emotions. An article published in the Journal of Personality and Social Psychology (2016) looks at the research carried out by Professor Igor

Grossmann from the psychology department at the University of Waterloo in Ontario.

Western cultures, specifically in parts of the world like Great Britain, the US, and Canada, where people are more self-oriented, tend to look at mixed feelings as undesirable. People who live in other-oriented cultures, such as Asia, experience much more complex emotions. They are able to differentiate their emotions better and balance them to enjoy emotionally rich experiences.

The research was extensive. It considered the frequency of mixed emotional expressions from 1.3 million websites and blogs combined with two other studies that involved mixed emotions during daily activities. Across all three studies, the results showed that those focusing on other people in their culture had greater emotional complexity (Grossman, 2016).

According to experts like Grossmann, if you consider that the prevalence of mental health issues is generally higher in Western cultures than in East Asian ones, it is due to the strong link between mixed emotions and mental health.

Larson felt that when we experience two emotions that are usually considered polar opposites, the positive emotion has a way of detoxifying the negative. Therefore, people are open to better experiences where the negative isn't blocked out. As we have seen, blocking, suppressing, and ignoring negative emotions only encourages them to become stronger.

How to start thinking in a healthy way

Let's look at nine powerful techniques that will help you create the right balance between positive and negative emotions so that mixed emotions benefit your life.

1. Becoming more empathetic

The studies show that when we start turning our focus towards those around us, we become more emotionally aware, accepting the good with the bad, and our mental health may improve.

This isn't to say that we are emotionally selfish or only concerned about ourselves. However, more often than not, we look at other people and wish our lives could be more like theirs because we are only shown the positive side.

Putting ourselves in other people's shoes and showing them compassion is essential if we are to encourage a society that doesn't push away the dark side of life.

When people experience difficult times, remember the phrases we looked at that should be used instead of toxic positivity. Don't just tell them that everything is going to be alright. Instead, let them know that you are there to offer a non-judgmental ear and then actively listen.

An excellent way to become more understanding and

compassionate is to be kind but for the right reasons. We can fall into the trap of people-pleasing kindness where we are nice just because we seek approval or are scared of saying no. Kindness shouldn't come at the cost of our own values. For genuine compassion to exist, there should be no ulterior reason.

Put it into practice

Do one thing today that will make someone else happy without feeling it's a burden or expecting something in return. Pay a stranger a compliment, remind a loved one why they are amazing, ask your elderly neighbor if they need anything while you are out and about. It doesn't have to be big, but it does have to be unconditional.

2. Create a positive mindset

I have always preferred the term positive mindset to positive thinking. Essentially, they are the same. But when people talk about positive thinking, it borders on toxic positivity. It's like one step away from saying "Think positive thoughts," even if you're swimming in a tank full of sharks.

A positive mindset is an emotional attitude where we approach our struggles and problems with optimism and expect a positive outcome. Of course, there is an element of positive thinking, but there is more to it:

- Acceptance—knowing that it's OK if something

doesn't turn out as we had hoped, and learning from the experience.

- Strength—being able to overcome our disappointment when things don't go as planned, and keep trying.

- Gratitude—seeking out the positive in life and being thankful for it (without telling yourself that it could be worse).

- Consciousness—being consciously aware and improving our levels of focus.

- Integrity—doing the right thing, being honest, and sticking to our morals, principles, and values.

Part of having a positive mindset is also to be happy and proud of our achievements. However, we also have to accept that we will have obstacles and challenges, but these aren't complete disasters nor road signs that dictate our future.

For many, to develop a positive mindset, we just need to slow down a little and smell the roses. Being constantly wired is not only draining, but it doesn't give us a chance to see or find the good in what would otherwise be just a bad situation.

For example, there should be mixed emotions when coming up to retirement age. They might worry about becoming older or not being around their colleagues. On the other hand, there will be more free time to do all the things they weren't able to. In this situation, and many like it, if we slow down, we realize there is a silver lining to even the most significant problems. But we need to look for it.

Nothing is ever all good or all bad. This mindset is known as cognitive distortion, and either negative bias or toxic positivity are getting in the way. You must remember this because when you are faced with a struggle, you will accept that there might be a negative aspect, but you can push yourself to work towards an optimistic outcome.

Put it into practice

Make a weekly tracking chart. In the first column, choose five of the following positive mindset behaviors. Track your week and see how many you can do daily. Repeat the next week, changing one or two behaviors or changing them all.

- Find the humor in a bad situation
- Be happy with what you have
- Envision a positive future
- Give more than you get
- Have a good time, laugh and smile
- Make someone else laugh or smile
- Be happy for someone else's achievements
- Appreciate a relationship more than a material good

- Let someone take advantage of your energy
- Be proud when someone's negativity doesn't bring you down
- Stand up for your beliefs
- Stand up for someone else's beliefs
- Transform your negative self-talk into positive self-talk

3. Critical thinking

How many times have you criticized yourself because you can't make a decision? Then, finally, after much deliberation, you choose an option. Still, ten minutes later, one of the powerful ways of thinking takes over, and you start worrying worry in case you have rushed into things and you are going to mess things up, or everything is going to go so well that you just need to sit back and enjoy the ride!

Adults make over 35,000 decisions a day (Inc., 2020). Luckily, most of them are relatively straightforward, like what to wear or what to eat. But even then, many of us will mull over these decisions. Knowing how to make the best decisions is part of healthy thinking, as it helps us eliminate potential flaws in our plan.

To improve our critical thinking skills, we first need to decide precisely what we want. For example, "I want to look good when choosing an outfit" is somewhat vague. To be more specific, you want an outfit that makes you look good and feel confident but is comfortable at the same time.

The same applies to food. "I want dinner." Well, of course, we all do! But based on your mood, you might want a dinner that is healthy, filling, easy to make. It's about being specific about your desired outcomes.

We all have biases. These attitudes come from our experiences and cultures. To make the right decision through critical thinking, we need to remove our biases, for example, never wanting to try Mexican food because your partner has told you it's all spicy.

Think of every decision from the perspective of the different people in your life. What would your parents tell you? How would your boss advise you? What words of wisdom would your friends give you?

Other people won't have the same biases as you. Even your siblings, who have been brought up in the same home will have their own experiences that give them a unique perspective on your problem.

At the same time as considering other people's advice, do your research. For example, choosing what to wear to an important meeting can be made easier by understanding the type of people who will be there. Are they older and more conservative? In that case, you might feel more comfortable in a suit.

Learning is an exceptional tool to make you feel more confident about your decisions.

Quite often, we fall into the trap of overcomplicating our decisions. Occam's razor is a mental model that reminds us that the simplest option is usually the best.

We complicate things when we add phrases like "But what if".

For example, let's say you have a problem, and you come up with a what-if for each solution and then a what-if for each of those. Before you know it, you have created ten more problems and forgotten the original one.

Put it into practice

Draw a tree trunk with three main branches and two smaller branches coming off each one. Write your problem in the tree trunk and your desired outcome at the top of the page.

On one tree trunk, write a solution based on what your gut tells you. On the second, the answer a loved one would offer you. On the third, the solution a professional would give you. On the smaller branches, write the pros and cons of each.

This visual mind map will help you structure your thoughts without adding multiple opinions and solutions and overcomplicating the process.

4. Solution-based thinking

A massive 77.3 percent of employers look for problem-solving skills in their candidates (Job Outlook, 2017). And this is only one of the skills required in the workplace. Problems arise in real life, something we must accept and try to prevent.

How does solution-based thinking help with healthy thinking? People who consider solutions before a difficulty arises are better able to handle a wide range of problems. They can think outside the box and develop ideas for themselves and others.

Solution-based thinking takes critical thinking to the next level because people know when a simple solution is needed or if the problem requires a more complex answer.

A solution-based thinker doesn't create more problems for others by solving their own problem. Furthermore, they will always look for a way to prevent a crisis by intervening when necessary.

To improve your solution-based thinking, go back to thinking like a novice. Experience teaches us so much, but it also closes particular doors. For example, in the first few weeks of a job, you have good and bad experiences — to help solve a problem. Because of this, you can look at more options.

After ten years on the job, you might come across a similar problem, and based on your past experiences; you will know which specific solutions to apply.

Another step up from critical thinking is that rather than focusing on the solutions to a problem, a solution-based thinker will aim to find the cause of this problem. Discovering the cause of a problem will not only help to come up with the most effective solution, but you will also help prevent the problem from happening in the future.

This takes us back to those wonderful words of wisdom, "Don't fix what isn't broken." Each day, we face options, problems, and challenges of all shapes and sizes. If this isn't enough, we try to make other things better. There is absolutely nothing wrong with this, but sometimes, when we try to make something better, we do the wrong thing, making things worse.

On the other hand, if we focus on what needs to be fixed, we can improve this area and, suddenly, many different aspects of life start to get better. Once you have discovered what works for you, you can keep doing more of the same. At the same time, things that aren't working can be changed.

Put it into practice

Be clear about the things that can't be changed and those that can. Instead of focusing on why these things can't be changed and coming up with extravagant ways to change them, ask yourself "how" questions.

You are currently working with a colleague who is nosey and inconsiderate. Negative thought patterns will only encourage you to dwell on this colleague, and you will dread going to work. Ignoring the problem and only looking at the bright side is toxic positivity. Spending time wishing to change your job is unrealistic.

• How can you make your working day more enjoyable?

• How can you talk to your colleague so that they understand how they are affecting you?

• How can you prepare yourself for the working day?

You can implement the following steps to make the necessary changes.

1. Take earphones so you can listen to music

2. Use an **"I"** statement to explain your feelings to your colleague

3. Begin the day with five minutes of meditation to feel more centered

5. Mindfulness

Once upon a time, I was a mindful skeptic. Things like meditation and yoga were simply ancient Buddhist traditions that enriched some people. Then, going through my very darkest moments, a therapist recommended I try taking a class (from a certified, experienced instructor who wasn't about to blurt toxic positivity).

Despite being ridiculed by my girlfriend (more toxic

behavior), I discovered that mindfulness was a potent tool that would help change my mindset.

It is now clear why Fortune 500 companies like General Mill, Google, and Apple implement mindfulness meditation as part of employee development.

Both science and experience have proven the benefits of mindfulness and meditation. For example, employees at a particular software and information technology corporation were offered seven weekly one-hour group sessions on loving-kindness meditation. They were also asked to meditate five times a week for fifteen-twenty minutes.

Employees experienced more positive emotions, a greater sense of purpose in life, decreased illness symptoms, and reduced depressive symptoms (Fredrickson et al., 2011).

Fifty-three participants in a study practiced body-scan meditation for twenty minutes a day to improve selflessness. Compared with the participants who only rested for twenty minutes, body scan meditation reduced anxiety levels and increased levels of happiness (Dambrun, 2018).

Despite its excellent benefits, there is still the issue of "too much of a good thing." Most experts believe that twenty minutes of mindfulness is sufficient to enjoy its benefits. What's more, excessive meditation can have adverse effects such as deteriorated sleep quality, moments of distress, distortion, and even panic attacks (BBC Worklife, 2020).

The right amount of mindfulness can help us to tune into our emotions. When we take the practice too far, it's like turning the volume of a subwoofer to the maximum. Your emotions are going to become extremely intense. Slight changes to our emotions may be more overwhelming than usual.

Extended periods of intense emotions can lead to emotional numbness. When this happens, we can't experience emotion—which will not allow for a fulfilling life.

Mindfulness is a simple concept but one that is much harder to practice. It is the ability to be fully present and aware of everything we do. For example, when we are with our children, our only concern is enjoying our time with them. When we exercise, we concentrate on what our senses tell us. When we rest—we rest!

But of course, what typically happens is that while we are doing one thing, we are thinking about what needs to be done and what hasn't been done. So, the past and future take away the present.

We can't afford to let the present slip past and not enjoy these incredible moments. But with busy minds, it's often hard to remain in the here and now. This is where mindfulness can help.

There are three main types of mindfulness practice: Meditation, which can be practiced sitting, standing, or walking. Second is meditation combined with other activities, most commonly yoga. And then, we have brief moments of mindfulness that we can add as part of our daily routine.

To successfully include mindfulness in your day, it is essential to start with short periods. It is easy for the mind to wander, and you don't want to become frustrated. You may also want to start in the same physical position to remind your brain that it is time for mindfulness. Try things like walking meditation when you can remain in the present.

Put it into practice

Find a comfortable, quiet spot where there will be no distractions. Sit, stand, or lie down, whatever feels right for you. Place your hands in your lap; you might also want to lower your chin slightly and close your eyes.

Take a slow, deep breath. Imagine this breath filling your lungs and belly, passing down your arms and legs to the tips of your fingers and toes. As you exhale, imagine this breath coming back through your hands and feet, moving out of your lungs and out of your body.

Continue to focus on your breathing. When a thought comes to your mind, don't ignore it or push it to one side. Notice it and accept it, but imagine it passing by you as if it were a cloud. Bring your focus back to your breathing.

Remember, only a few minutes at first. You may want to practice two or three times a day but never push yourself. If you become distracted, stop and try again a little later.

6. Self-care

There are several misconceptions when it comes to self-care. Some feel it is a hippy concept, and others are under the impression that it is just a different way to be indulgent or selfish. Nothing could be further from the truth.

Self-care is "the ability of individuals, families, and communities to promote health, prevent disease, maintain health, and to cope with illness and disability with or without the support of a healthcare provider." (World Health Organization, n.d.)

Based on this definition, self-care includes everything from proper hygiene practices to prevent illness to eating well and managing stress. So when you look at self-care from this point of view, you can see that self-care is essential now, more than ever.

Paula Gill Lopez PhD, an associate professor and chair of the Psychological and Educational Consultation Department at Fairfield University, Connecticut, said, "We have an epidemic of anxiety and depression." It's impossible to imagine healthy thinking if you aren't taking care of yourself.

Furthermore, it's impossible to imagine taking care of

others if you aren't at your best both physically and mentally.

A study published in BMC Medical Education showed how practicing self-care lowered the risk of higher stress levels. Eight hundred seventy-one medical students were asked to fill out online questionnaires to determine how self-care impacted the relationship between quality of life and stress. This relationship was weaker for those students who engaged in self-care, both in terms of physical anxiety and psychological stress (Ayala et al., 2018).

There are five core areas to self-care. We will look at each one and some additional ideas to improve your self-care practices.

Emotional self-care—not seeing emotions as good or bad, but just as they are, then choosing to react in either a good or bad way and accepting our negative emotions.

- Expressing our emotions in the right way

- Not letting others tell us how we should feel

- Talking openly about how we feel

- Crying and laughing when we need to and without guilt

Social self-care—strengthening our relationships with others. Whether you are an introvert or an extrovert, you need some form of social interaction.

- Catching up with people who you haven't seen for a while

- Keeping in touch with those who live far away

- Taking up new hobbies and interests to meet new people

- Putting an end to your toxic relationships

Sensory self-care—discovering ways to calm your mind, letting go of the past and future worries to experience the present.

- Focusing on your breathing and what you can smell

- Appreciating how the water feels in the shower or even at the sea or river

- Taking in the flavor of each bite of food you take

- Stroking pets

- Enjoying the warmth of the sun or the freshness of the rain on your face

Physical self-care—taking care of your body in terms of healthy habits, fitness, and diet.

- Eating a balanced diet with plenty of vitamins and nutrients

- Getting the right amount of different types of exercise

- Getting enough sleep

- Understanding your limits and knowing when to rest

Spiritual self-care—spiritual self-care doesn't imply religion. If you don't believe in a higher power, you still have values and beliefs that require attention.

- Practicing mindfulness

- Learning about world religions, practices, and cultures to take inspiration

- Being grateful

- Using affirmations

Put it into practice

A good habit takes six weeks to establish as part of your routine. You don't want to make too many changes and not keep up with them. You won't be able to feel the long-term benefits. So instead, start by asking yourself four key questions:

1. Where am I at this point in my life?

2. Who am I?

3. What are my values, my principles, my ethics?

4. Where do I want to take my life?

With the answers to these questions, you will be able to prioritize your self-care needs and start introducing one or two new practices at a time.

7. Stoic exercises

Stoicism is a school of philosophy that dates back to ancient Greece and Rome. For example, Zeno of Citium became shipwrecked near Athens. Rather than seeing this as a misfortune, he turned it into a positive by learning the predominant philosophies in that area—turning his negative into a positive.

Today, stoicism is seen as a way of living your life as best as possible—it reminds us of what is of real value to us. It is a widespread practice, used by the likes of Warren Buffet and Bill Gates, to find peace and build a stronger character.

The history of Stoicism is rich, and there are numerous different practices. It is worth investigating the philosophy, especially if you are interested in cognitive behavioral therapy as it has made its way into this modern practice. We will go over some practices that encourage healthy thinking.

Put it into practice

1. A view from above—guided meditations that can help with this. Choose a spot in the distance; it could be from another planet or star or just from above the clouds. Look down on the world and take in everything you see. Don't make judgments—just be an observer,

This practice helps you see the bigger picture in life and how insignificant parts of our lives are compared with this bigger picture.

2. Guard your time— if you lose $100, you can get it back. If you say goodbye to a toxic relationship, make space for new, healthier relationships. The one thing you will never get back is time. How you use this precious resource will impact your happiness.

What do you get out of spending thirty minutes on social media? When you waste time procrastinating, what do you have to show? If you give your time to those who don't appreciate it, you are handing over an asset that you could otherwise use for the greater good.

3. Don't succumb to the paradox of choice— since the technology boom, we are presented with more and more choices. So many that we can often become paralyzed by the available options. Options are always good, but not when they stop you from making a decision.

For example, there were nineteen stoic philosophers before 180 AD, each with their own practices. If I listed all of these practices, you would be overwhelmed with options and spend more time deliberating the best ones to choose. For this reason, I have given you three!

8. Intelligent action

Intelligence is incorrectly measured in grades, credentials, and even bank account size. However, intelligence is based on one's actions. Even those with high IQs can completely lack common sense or emotional intelligence and do the wrong things. If you are truly intelligent, you act intelligently.

One of the smartest ways we can act intelligently is to create goals and take action to achieve these goals.

You might be familiar with setting SMART goals. SMART goals was created by George Doran, Arthur Miller, and James Cunningham in 1981. Since then, setting goals is no longer seen as reserved for corporations but a tool we can all use to act intelligently.

Goals should be **S**pecific. This means you need to give as much detail as you can about what you want to achieve. They have to be **M**easurable, so add detail to the specifics by adding numbers. If you have the resources to achieve your goals, they are **A**ttainable; if not, what resources do you need? Goals need to be **R**ealistic. Setting unrealistic goals is setting yourself up for failure. Finally, they must be **T**imely, so there needs to be a deadline.

When it comes to toxic positivity, we can often get confused between a goal and a dream. We dream about having a particular object or reaching a goal, which causes the brain to activate the reward system and release dopamine. This is a lovely feel-good moment, but we must follow up to attain the goal.

Of course, we should think big when setting goals. There has to be a challenge behind the goal. But, if the goal is unrealistic, there is the potential for more harm. You will be setting yourself up for a long road of failures.

If we look back at the case of Emma, who put off her

goal to have a horse, it wasn't because the goal was unrealistic. It's just that the plan wasn't in place because there was no "healthy dreaming."

She loved horses and wanted to own one. If she had started with small steps, like taking riding lessons, her brain would have released the dopamine reward, keeping her on track to the next steps in the bigger plan.

Once you have decided on your SMART goals, it's time to work on a step-by-step plan to achieve them. This often means breaking down goals into bite-sized actions.

Each action should have a reward, which will motivate you to stay focused on the long-term goal. The goal, the steps, and the rewards should all be written down and, even better, shared with others. This way, you are more accountable for your goals.

Sometimes, as we have all seen recently, something will happen that prevents us from achieving our goals. Goals can't be set in stone to the extent that we can't adjust them.

Imagine you have ten real things on your to-do list, but the school phones to let you know your child is sick. Or your work goals depend on a colleague finishing their part of a task.

You need to be able to readjust your goals, so review your long- and short-term goals continuously to ensure they stay realistic and attainable.

Put it into practice

Here is an example of a bad goal and a SMART goal that will lead to action.

Bad goal—I want to lose weight.

SMART goal- I want to lose five kilos in ten weeks. To do this, I will start by cutting out sweets, chocolate, and fast food and start exercising three times a week for thirty minutes. After two weeks, I will increase this to five times a week for forty minutes. My reward will be a chocolate donut for every two kilos I lose and two new pairs of trousers after five kilos. I'm going to post this on Facebook so that I commit to this goal.

9. Choose M.A.D.

I have become cautious about the advice I take, but I was intrigued when someone told me about M.A.D. Wasn't there enough madness in the world?

M.A.D. is very simple. It stands for Make a Difference. And if you commit to making a difference each day, you will not only start thinking in a healthy way, but you will also know that you are continuously working towards a better life.

Put it into practice

There are so many ways you can make a difference. Try to create a balance between making a difference in other people's lives and your own. Here are just a few ideas:

- Be respectful
- Show up on time
- Sponsor a child
- Pay it forward
- Clean out a cupboard or your wardrobe
- Declutter your computer
- Share your experiences with those who need help
- Make eye contact and share a smile
- Donate blood—one pint of blood can save three lives!
- Apologize from the heart when necessary
- Babysit for a single parent
- Cook extra food and freeze it so you can have a night off
- Stop comparing yourself to others
- Have a spring clean
- Get a haircut
- Turn off your phone for thirty minutes
- Put some water out for stray animals

Positive thinking is a good thing, but only if we are realistic. It takes time to change your mindset, and there is a vast difference between the two extremes.

This chapter has covered nine techniques to achieve healthy thinking, from changing your mindset to creating goals that aren't simply wishes but are specific, planned actions. So, rather than aiming straight for positive thinking, set yourself a realistic goal to achieve healthy thinking.

Nine doesn't sound like a huge number, but it will still be too many for most people to begin all at once. So how do you choose the best techniques to start with? The ones that are going to be easiest and that will become a habit.

For example, a great place to start is self-care and setting goals. This will give you the strength, motivation, and vision to help you with critical thinking or solution-based thinking.

Healthy thinking is closely associated with emotional management. It's a bit of a chicken and egg scenario—without a firm grasp on emotions, the ability to think in a healthy way is going to be all the more complex and vice-versa. The beginning of the next chapter will go over just how incredible and complex the brain and our emotions are.

CHAPTER 5: HOW TO MASTER YOUR EMOTIONS

When I tell people that I research a topic, they often assume I read a few studies or articles, and that's it. On the contrary, I did a vast amount of research on the topic of emotions and was absolutely fascinated with the subject. And I confess, I have watched Disney Pixar's *Inside Out* several times—in the name of research.

Whether it's thanks to those classic Disney films and other similar cartoons, fairy tales, and 80s love ballads, people can still be swept away by the notion that the heart controls our emotions and the brain our logic and intelligence. Even when we know this makes no sense.

What are emotions, and how is the brain involved?

In the most basic sense of the word, our emotions have enabled humankind to survive. They are there to warn us of danger. We wouldn't have survived very long if cave dwellers had sat around and debated the best solution to the giant saber-toothed tiger eyeing up its next meal. They needed that fight or flight response.

As man evolved, so did emotions. What separated humans from, say, reptiles was the development of a third nervous system, known as the Polyvagal theory, which we will come back to in a bit.

Our brain contains many structures and systems. It's the limbic system that is responsible for our emotions and behavior. The two most important parts of the limbic system are the hippocampus and the amygdala.

The hippocampus is where memories are formed and then filed and stored in different areas of the brain, most of which are in the long-term memory. The hippocampus can connect with stimuli such as smells linked to other memories. It is also an essential part of the brain for developing new brain cells.

New neurons are also made in the amygdala. The amygdala is vital for our emotional responses but is also linked to the emotions attached to different memories, especially fear. Another function of the amygdala is to determine the strength of the stored memories. Only a few repetitions of fear are required to form a memory, fewer than some of our more positive emotions, so these memories tend to be stronger.

The hypothalamus receives input from our limbic system

and then passes the messages on to our autonomic nervous system. This unconscious system was thought to be composed of different structures, including the sympathetic and parasympathetic nervous systems.

The sympathetic nervous system is what we consider to be our fight or flight system. It prepares the body to cope with fear or stress. Our breath quickens, our heart rate increases, and we experience a rush of adrenaline.

The parasympathetic nervous system then acts to relax the body. Stephen Porges put forward a theory that is now widely accepted among mental health professionals today. The Polyvagal theory came about after Porges's experiments with the vagus nerve system.

The Polyvagal theory states that there is a third three-part nervous system, also known as the social engagement system. This system allows us to enter social situations that would typically have been assessed as dangerous.

Reading facial expressions and body language is crucial. Before any word is spoken, we are accessing the emotions of others. We subconsciously read cues from other people and the parasympathetic nervous system reacts along with the sympathetic system.

That's a lot of science, so let's take a look at an example.

You are walking down a dark street at night; it's not a great area. You hear footsteps behind you. This auditory message gets sent to the limbic system, where numerous chemicals are released.

These chemicals are the message that will trigger the sympathetic nervous system into action, and you run. Finally, you make it to a place of safety, the danger passes, your parasympathetic system kicks in and tells your body to calm down.

Many experts will agree that it's impossible to tie our emotions and behavior down to one or two systems because our emotions are complex. For example, we haven't considered how nerves make us feel sick.

The key takeaway here is that it would be naive to think that singing "Always look on the bright side of life" will control our emotions.

The complexity of our emotions

Here is a little exercise to do before we look at how complex our emotions are. Take a moment to write down the names of all the emotions you can think of. Once you have finished, check to see how many of those emotions are negative.

You might be shocked to discover that more negative emotions are on your list than positive ones. This isn't your fault. As we saw in the previous section, it is easier for negative emotions such as fear to be more embedded in our memories.

Every time we think about something, the synapses in the

brain strengthen, and the memory becomes stronger. As a result, we tend to reflect more on our negative experiences than our positive ones, making these memories stronger and easier to recall. This is known as our negativity bias.

As part of my own research, I performed the same activity and came up with fifty-eight. However, in total, there are 34,000 emotions!

To get our heads around this extensive list of emotions, American scientist Robert Plutchik devised the emotional wheel. Our eight basic emotions are in the center of the wheel; each one stems out as the severity increases.

- Vigilance-anticipation-interest
- Ecstasy-joy-serenity
- Admiration-trust- acceptance
- Terror-fear-apprehension
- Amazement-surprise-distraction
- Grief-sadness-pensiveness
- Loathing-disgust-boredom
- Rage-anger-annoyance

(Plutchik, 2001)

Multiple emotions can be combined between these stems, supporting the concept that our feelings are mixed. For example, between the extremes of sadness and disgust, people can feel remorse. Between joy and trust, there is love.

By taking a look at anger alone, we can feel or be:

- Let down–betrayed/resentful
- Humiliated–disrespected/ridiculed
- Bitter–indignant/violated
- Mad–furious/jealous
- Aggressive–provoked/hostile
- Frustrated–infuriated/annoyed
- Distant–withdrawn/numb
- Critical–skeptical/dismissive

And so, the wheel continues to expand as each emotion can be mixed with another to form a different feeling. And this is how we get to 34,000 emotions. But there is more. What happens when we think about the emotions we have about our emotions?

What are second-order emotions?

Last week, Kate was having a hard time with her partner. They had argued about where they were going to spend the Christmas vacations. As she talked to her friend about this, she replied, "Be grateful you have a boyfriend."

Initially, Kate felt awful because she wanted to go away and escape the usual Christmas stress. However, her partner wanted time with the family. She felt selfish and needed to talk about this to gain a better perspective.

This feeling of selfishness, shame, and confusion were Kate's primary emotions— already enough to deal with! When her friend told her that she should be thankful she wasn't alone, the shame grew into guilt, and she experienced second-order emotions or meta-emotions.

There are four types of meta-emotions:

- negative-negative—feeling bad about feeling bad
- negative-positive—feeling bad about feeling good
- positive-positive—feeling good about feeling good
- positive-negative—feeling good about feeling bad

This is incredibly overwhelming. First, you have a system in the brain that is made up of other systems that control your emotions. Then you have a set of emotions sparked by your original emotions, and there are potentially 34,000 different labels between them.

Emotions will also vary depending on cognition and our thoughts about certain situations. In some cultures, a man shaking a woman's hand will spark a range of negative emotions, whereas, in other cultures, it is appropriate behavior. A joke can be hilarious in one country and rude in another.

But what if we peel back all these layers and simplify the problem. Behind these thousands of emotions, there is a system. You are not the system. It is part of your brain. Various parts of the brain can create new brain cells in a process called neuroplasticity. So, rather than seeing emotions as a form of survival that is no longer so necessary, we need to separate ourselves from them and recognize that they are a system that can be changed.

One of the first steps to emotional management is to see the difference between "I am angry" and "I feel anger". I am angry implies a permanent state of anger. I feel anger separates your body from your emotional system.

Emotions are not our enemy

There is negativity bias; fear is more easily stored in our memories, depression and anxiety are on the rise. Wouldn't it be easier not to block these emotions but simply not to have them?

'Elliot', a famous patient of the neuroscientist Antonio Damasio would disagree. Elliot had a brain tumor that was removed during surgery. At the same time, part of the frontal lobe had to be removed. Elliot's IQ wasn't affected—he was still intelligent. However, he was utterly incapable of showing any emotion. He was unable to make decisions and became disengaged from the world.

Despite Elliot's high IQ, his marriage and professional life were destroyed. Finally, Damasio made a bold statement that would go against the teachings of people like Descartes, Plato, and Kant. These past greats had stated that the best decisions are made when we ignore emotions and focus on rational processing.

Mastering your emotions in six steps

As I have said, I am careful of whose advice I take, but the words neurologist, psychologist, and Holocaust survivor, Viktor E. Frankel are too powerful to ignore.

"Between stimulus and response there is a space. In that space is our power to choose our response. In our response lies our growth and our freedom".

You can't control other people's emotions or behavior, nor is it your responsibility to do so. Still, it is up to you to decide what to do in that split second between emotion and response. Managing your emotions includes recognizing them and controlling them so that you can follow with the appropriate actions.

1. Label your emotions

You will probably identify eight basic emotions: anger, fear, sadness, disgust, surprise, anticipation, trust, and fear. But there are a possible 34,000 descriptions one can use, and these eight labels are not specific enough.

You can be *surprised* by watching the news or *surprised* by a gift from your partner—the two are unlikely to be the same. Labeling your exact emotions is a technique used in Dialectical Behavior Therapy and helps people cope with the complex emotions they experience.

2. Understand that emotions are neither good nor bad

Shakespeare wrote, "There is nothing either good or bad, but thinking makes it so." The same can be said of our emotions. Labeling them is necessary to understand them. But only when you think an emotion is good or bad does it become that way.

If you are scared of leaving your home right now, the emotion isn't bad. It is there to protect you, just as it did our distant ancestors. However, the action of not being able to leave your home is what is destructive.

We call them negative emotions not because they are nasty or dirty words. It's because they have a negative impact on your life. Take lust, for example. It's just a word that can lead to unique experiences or, if you are unable to control them, negative experiences. Accepting this is the first step in accepting your emotions.

3. Recognize your emotional patterns

Sometimes, this is relatively easy. When your kids constantly interrupt you, you feel the frustration building up. When your boss manipulates you into working overtime, you feel gullible.

Other times, it isn't so easy. For example, your thinking

towards an activity or person may have become stuck. For example, if you dread meeting a specific person at every social occasion, there is an emotional pattern even though it might not always be as bad as you imagine.

Emotional patterns that are stuck in your head mean you can't change the outcome until you break the habit.

4. Break the cycle of emotional patterns

Scenarios may change, but you will notice the cycle of emotional patterns remains the same. You feel jealous of your boyfriend or girlfriend in high school, your next partner in university, you get married, become jealous again. You are on a roundabout and can't see get off.

The critical fact is that although the scenario is different, we still go through the same repetitive motion. If it's your boss, you may have been too emotionally drained to stand up to the manipulation last time, or you weren't prepared. Your husband or wife is not the same teenager you thought you had fallen in love with back at school.

So far, we have spoken about what-ifs in a negative way because they cause us to ruminate endlessly. Now, we will look at what-ifs in a positive way.

What if you talked to your partner today and explained how you felt. You tell them that you feel insecure although they haven't done anything wrong. Rather than being bitter, they might find ways to reassure you, and the cycle is broken.

What if today, you simply said "No" or told your boss, "That's not going to work for me."

What if you tried asking your child to put their hand on your arm when they wanted your attention instead of constantly interrupting you.

Now that you have recognized your emotional patterns, you can look at the what-ifs that will lead to positive outcomes.

5. Create some distance between you and your emotions

I am not suggesting you should ignore your feelings. There is a right and wrong time to deal with them. If you feel like your emotions are too powerful, it's not the right time to say no to your boss. Your message won't be assertive but more likely aggressive.

Create some emotional space—this can be a short walk to experience the calming effect of nature, looking at pictures of friends and family, watching that amusing video, or maybe just talking to someone else.

6. Express your emotions in the right way

There is an incredibly short time between emotion and action, so expressing your feelings correctly takes practice. It also often takes some time to organize your thoughts, so don't say something in the heat of the moment.

Step away if you cannot organize your thoughts in that split second. Instead, say something like, "I will get back to you on that," and walk away. Then, decide the outcome you want, prepare the phrases you need and go back at a more appropriate time to say what you want.

Always go back to say what you want to say. If you don't, you can't break the cycle, and you will end up feeling regret and other meta-emotions.

How to handle meta-emotions

As with our primary emotions, the first step to handling our send-order or meta-emotions is to uncover how we feel about them.

To do this, you need to ask questions such as:

- How do I feel about being happy?

- How do I feel when others are excited?

- How do I feel when I am angry?

- How do I feel about being anxious?

- How do I feel when other people are proud?

Just like our primary emotions, meta-emotions have an essential role to play. For example, if you are treated unfairly, you might at first feel disappointed, then anger — anger is the natural meta-emotion. Without anger, you wouldn't have the necessary motivation to change the situation.

What is this guilt telling you if you feel guilty during a proud moment? You may have stepped on someone else's toes to achieve your goal, or perhaps you did something that went against your values.

Also analyze these meta-emotions and decide if they are warranted. For example, if you didn't step on anyone's toes or go against your values, perhaps you are comparing yourself to those less fortunate. This isn't fair on you because you worked hard for your proud moment. In this case, you need to go back to self-care and treat yourself with a little more kindness.

Don't forget the power of an apology. Your meta-emotions could be warning you that you are in the wrong. If this is the case, a sincere apology will go a long way to making amends and understanding these meta-emotions.

Keeping an emotional journal

We have looked at how beneficial journals can be in general. Emotional journals are also helpful. When we write about our feelings, we learn to prioritize our problems and concerns.

If you can take five or ten minutes at the end of the day to write about the emotions you have felt throughout that day, you will be in a better situation to recognize the patterns and the triggers.

Here are six steps to keeping an emotional journal:

1. Name your primary emotion

2. Define the cause

3. Decide if there were any meta-emotions

4. List any action this emotion caused you to take

5. Check to see if the emotion was appropriate and justified

6. Brainstorm alternative ways to handle the situation better

Negative-negative meta-emotions are the most common. Unfortunately, they can also be the hardest to handle, leading to other mental health issues like stress, anxiety, and depression. If you can't control your negative-negative or positive-negative meta-emotions, it is worth consulting a doctor to see if therapy will help.

Put it into practice

The steps above are ongoing, leading to increased emotional awareness and better emotional management. Next, we will look at some methods to help stimulate your parasympathetic nervous system to induce calm.

- Get plenty of green leafy vegetables. They are rich in Vitamin B, C, E, and magnesium, all of which are good for your nervous system.

- Avocados, nuts, and salmon, even dark chocolate are

anti-stress foods that support the parasympathetic nervous system.

• Focus on deep, abdominal breathing to rebalance the oxygen and carbon dioxide in your body.

• Practice visualization. Imagine a happy, calm, or soothing place. Be specific, activate all of your senses and imagine what you can smell, hear, see and feel.

• Meditate. Take a few minutes to relax, be comfortable, and bring your attention back to the present.

• Be mindful. Take a step back from all of the tasks you are trying to achieve and focus on just one.

• Focus on a word that calms you down. It doesn't have to be related to emotions or positivity. Just a word that rolls off your tongue and that you like the sound of.

• Imagine what is going on in your body. Sometimes, our brains are going so fast that it is hard to focus on any specific technique. For example, I have always found it helpful to imagine the mailman taking a message from my eyes and knocking on the door of the limbic system. The limbic system then phones the hypothalamus, which shouts out the window to the nervous system.

• Run one or two fingers lightly over your lips. Your lips have parasympathetic fibers throughout them. Touching the lips activates your parasympathetic nervous system. Be careful who is watching—you don't want to send the wrong message!

This chapter has covered the importance and range of our emotions and how they can be managed. The science is simply fascinating, so please take the time just to sit and think about how amazing your brain and your body are.

More often than not, we see some of our emotions as being a nuisance or hindrance when, in fact, they are incredibly beneficial.

Nevertheless, emotions that cause negativity are highly destructive. Therefore, it might require a greater effort to manage your emotions and begin thinking in a healthy way. If you feel that your negative thinking is impeding your progress, the next chapter will provide simple methods to teach you how to control negative emotions.

CHAPTER 6: IT'S OK NOT TO BE OK — SIMPLE TRICKS TO COPE WITH YOUR NEGATIVE EMOTIONS

It's incredible how these poor negative emotions have managed to get such a bad reputation. Even when we understand negativity bias and mixed emotions, we still look at negative feelings as dirty words that shouldn't be allowed out in public.

The first thing to get our heads around here is that negative emotions are not destructive. We have already mentioned this, but it's worth repeating! Every emotion serves a purpose. We might not always know its purpose, and this is when we start to feel emotions are negative.

The truth is, emotions are neither good nor bad. It's what you do with them that counts and will lead to positive or negative outcomes.

We will use disappointment as an example. You receive feedback on a project, and it isn't what you had hoped. You feel disappointed. You could look at this as a sign of failure. But, alternatively, you could look at the feeling of disappointment as an incentive for growth and a motivation to improve your skills.

Anger is another example. If you are angry and take it out on others, it becomes a negative emotion. But, on the other hand, if you use your anger to fix a wrong, the feeling of anger is a positive emotion.

Let's take a closer look at some of our perceived negative emotions. Please remember that we are not saying that these emotions are good or bad. However, in the following cases, even a vestige of emotion can lead to positive results.

Why do we get angry?

Anger goes back to our survival instincts. If we take a closer look at the fight or flight response, our ability to fight is fueled by anger. It heightens our senses and keeps us vigilant and focused. This need to protect ourselves can also be energizing.

We are angry when something prevents us from getting what we want or need. However, the right measure of this emotion can encourage us to resolve problems to overcome obstacles and, therefore, help us achieve our goals. When looked at in this context, anger can lead us to self-improvement.

There is a lot of injustice in the world and not only against us. By feeling angry about unfairness, we are more inclined to do something about it. We have seen this on a global scale with climate control. It wasn't until masses of everyday people started getting angry that governments began to take action. So, in this sense, anger helps us defend our values and beliefs.

Can sadness really be beneficial?

Sadness has, in the past, been harder to understand because it doesn't play a role in our flight or fight response, so it's difficult to see how it has helped human evolution. Happiness is still preferred over sadness, but MRI images of the brain have shown that mild sadness can be beneficial in more ways than one.

Joseph P. Forgas and colleagues (2014) conducted various studies on sadness.

In one study, individuals had a better recollection of objects they had seen in a shop on dark rainy days that made people feel sad than on sunny days. Attention to detail and memory were boosted.

The team were also able to prove that sadness leads to better judgment. When groups of happy and sad people were asked to rate the likely truth of fifty trivia statements, the sad group was better able to determine which phrases were true. Negative moods reduce judgmental bias. It can help us see how things really are rather than seeing things through happy rose-colored glasses.

Sadness may also increase the motivation and effort we put into tasks. When people are happy, they don't need to make an effort to improve their mood. On the other hand, sad people need to make an effort to enhance their mood, and this effort can be reflected in other activities.

In certain situations, sadness has been seen to improve interactions. For example, after a group of people had watched a sad film and others a happy movie, they were asked to retrieve a film from the next-door office. It was noted that the sad people were more polite.

Is loneliness that bad?

We have probably all been feeling lonelier since the pandemic began. But in fact, loneliness comes in all shapes and sizes. You don't need to be confined to your home to be lonely. You might be living in a country in a strange land where you don't understand the language. You may feel lonely when you feel left out of a conversation.

Loneliness goes back to our survival instincts and the hunter-gather days. When people began to feel lonely, it reminded them that it was time to go back to the group. In a group setting, we have the chance to feel validated and prove our worth.

It's essential to keep telling yourself that being alone isn't the same as being lonely, despite sometimes feeling lonely when you are by yourself. This time alone can be beneficial to regroup our thoughts, like soul-searching and deciding on the things we still want to achieve.

Moreover, lonely times often push us to become more sociable again. We saw this with COVID-19. After weeks and months of isolation, loneliness was at its peak for many people all over the world.

It made us realize that our relationships were more important than we had ever imagined. Many started contacting friends and family again. It was heartwarming to see neighbors joining from balconies and windows to show appreciation and connect.

What can we learn from disappointment?

Much like loneliness, COVID-19 left many of us repeatedly disappointed. Weddings, holidays, family get-togethers have all been postponed or canceled. Business expansion has been put on hold, as have promotions, etc.

Like the other so-called negative emotions, disappointment can be good or bad, depending on what we take from it. However, if we dwell on the negative, we will find that disappointment will be centered on what we missed or the expectations that weren't met.

In his book, Atomic Habits, 2018, James Clear described this as the "Valley of Disappointment." When we set ourselves a goal, we have a degree of expectation related to achieving that goal. Unfortunately, there is a dip where our disappointment doesn't meet our expectations before we have a breakthrough goal.

For example, someone has set a goal of saving $1,000 in three months. They are excited about this and have a plan lined up. However, there will be disappointment from the moment they set the goal to reaching it. It will be harder to stick to your goal if you let negativity mix with this valley of disappointment.

As disappointment occurs regularly in life, we need to see them as beneficial. Our resilience is tested when passing through this "valley of disappointment". It provides an opportunity for self-growth and a chance to become tougher instead of being tempted to give up when things get tough.

Another simple way of looking at disappointment as beneficial is recognizing that disappointment implies passion for something. If there are no feelings of disappointment, it's because you didn't care enough to start with. As in our previous example, the $1,000 goal wasn't enough to get you excited.

The combination of anxiety, worry, and nerves

We have talked about these three emotions and fear to some extent. These emotions are crucial for our survival, and although we aren't faced with the same dangers as our ancestors, we still need these emotions to make us aware of the potential risks we encounter today.

When we are overcome with anxiety or fear, we need to recognize what our body tells us. Is it saying that we need to protect ourselves from something? Or do we need to use these emotions to take action?

If you have been stuck in the same job for some time, you might fear putting yourself out there, getting noticed, or asking for that promotion. However, this isn't the time to freeze or run away. Instead, it's time to use this emotion as the momentum to push for a promotion—for your own happiness in the long run.

What is the difference between guilt and shame?

At one point, guilt was seen as a public emotion and shame as a private one, but since the 1970s, the two have been defined more accurately. Shame is an emotion we turn onto ourselves, whereas guilt is turned onto others. So even though they are different, you can feel guilt and shame over the same action.

If you go out drinking one night and can't pull yourself out of bed for the kids' soccer match, you feel shame about the drinking and lack of self-control. However, you feel guilty for not being there for your children.

Both guilt and shame allow us to analyze our behavior and decide if our actions require an apology. There are other ways we can use these seemingly negative emotions to help us.

Feeling guilt is an empathetic trait. It shows that we can

see things from other people's perspectives and see the pain or suffering we have caused. For example, a group of volunteers was asked to read facial expressions and identify anger, sadness, happiness, fear, disgust, or shame. The volunteers who were more prone to guilt were the ones who could more accurately recognize emotions in others (Treeby, 2015). This highlights the link between guilt and empathy.

Shame is another emotion that plays a part in the survival of the species. It teaches us about the social norms of living in groups. For example, if one person in the group was caught stealing, it created a problem within the group dynamics, such as a lack of trust. To survive, a group had to be able to rely on one another.

Much like anger and fear, shame isn't as important today, but it is still necessary for people across all cultures to understand what is considered right and wrong. Stealing your flatmate's last frozen yogurt won't reduce your chances of survival, but it still goes against social norms.

How envy and jealousy differ

Let's tackle these separately, starting with jealousy. Jealousy is a feeling we have when we want something others have. There is often a degree of resentment and sometimes suspicion. One of the purest examples of jealousy is when a sibling has to get used to sharing parents' attention after the arrival of a new sibling.

The roots of jealousy are more likely to be fear of loss. In the case of the older sibling, they fear that the baby will get more attention or, at least, take away some of the attention that was theirs.

If you feel jealous, it doesn't make you a bad person. However, you need to get to the bottom of your fear of loss. If not, it could turn into negative behavior such as false praise and knowingly giving bad advice. Nevertheless, there is still a purpose.

On the other hand, envy is wanting what someone else has but at the same time feeling pleased for their achievements. For example, if you are jealous of a colleague who got the promotion you were hoping for, you may picture them messing up on day one. Being envious means you are disappointed that you didn't get the job, but you wish them well.

We can use the disappointment that comes with envy because, instead of thinking of ways to sabotage the other person, we will look for ways to work harder to achieve the same. Combine passion with envy, and you have two essential tools for self-improvement.

Why grief is a necessary emotion

Grief is commonly met with toxic positivity, not necessarily because the other person is trying to cheer you up but because they don't know what to say to improve things. We hear things like, "They are in a better place" or "At least they aren't suffering anymore." These kind words do little to comfort us.

Grief is not a pleasant emotion, but at the same time, we have to accept that there will be times when we will experience it, and blocking or ignoring it will make life much harder.

We tend to assume that grief is felt when a loved one dies, but it can occur in many situations, such as:

- The end of a relationship
- The loss of health, job, or home
- A miscarriage
- The death of a pet
- The loss of safety, security, or stability

It's hard to imagine a positive side to grief, but we can take lessons from it. Of course, working through the stages of grief (denial, anger, bargaining, depression, and acceptance) at your own pace is part of the process. But it does help to understand other things we can gain from grieving.

Sadly, there comes a great deal of acceptance with grief. We have to accept that there are things out of our control, and it helps us be grateful, not only for what we have but, more importantly, for the things that we can control. Grief also allows us to reflect on and appreciate the person or situation we have lost.

The five stages of grief allow us to look closer and understand our emotions. With this comes greater emotional intelligence. We can learn more about ourselves as well as others. If you can deal with grief in a healthy way, your goals may become more apparent, and you develop a new sense of determination.

Grief is the perfect example of when it is OK not to be OK. Everybody handles grief differently, but it is essential to listen to your feelings to reduce the risk of grief evolving into something more serious. Life is short, but that doesn't mean you need to push aside these feelings and achieve all your dreams in an instant.

Whether you once viewed emotions as negative or positive, each one has two functions. The first is to provide you with information about the situation; the second is to guide your behavior. For these two reasons alone, we need to listen to them.

With strong emotions like fear, envy, and guilt, it is OK not to be OK while you process the information that your brain has received and decide on the appropriate behavior.

However, the moment you start to develop negative meta-emotions about these primary emotions, there is a strong chance that the negativity will take over your decision-making abilities.

To stop both the primary and meta-emotions from taking control, we need to learn how to deal with them successfully before they manifest into something worse.

How to handle emotions so they don't result in adverse outcomes

Your partner has cheated on you, your kids have told you they hate you, or maybe your boss has humiliated you in front of the entire office. Rage is the only thing that comes to mind. Should you just count to ten and move on because tomorrow will be a better day?

No! You have every right to feel this rage. But now it's all about what you do with it. Are you going to set your partner's clothes on fire? Tell your kids that they are ungrateful and slam a few doors? Teach your boss a lesson and quit? These actions will release the rage, but they aren't going to solve the original problem. The chances are, they will make it worse.

It all goes back to that split second between the emotion and the reaction. This split-second deserves more credit than we ever give it, and although it may seem impossible to overcome such strong feelings in the blink of an eye, it is indeed possible and necessary.

Let's look at five ways to handle these powerful emotions, even when you think it's impossible.

1. Stimulate your parasympathetic nervous system

Often, you will hear that the first step to managing emotions is to understand their cause. This is undoubtedly true, but there isn't enough time for this internal dialogue if we go back to the split second between the emotion and reaction.

We need solutions that will calm us down before we react instantly. To do this, we can stimulate our parasympathetic nervous systems to start telling the body to calm down.

There is an excellent reason why people count to ten and breathe deeply. This controlled action sends signals to the brain to help it understand that the immediate threat is no longer there.

The vagus nerve also has a significant role in calming us down. You can jolt the vagus nerve into action by splashing cold water on your face. You can also massage the vagus nerve. The AllCEUs Counseling Education channel has a fantastic video explaining the vagus nerve and how to massage it.

I can't stress enough that these three techniques are to be used in the moment so that you feel calmer and more emotionally balanced to face the situation in front of you. Just because you start to feel more relaxed doesn't mean that your emotions are now under control. So whether it's ten minutes, an hour, or five hours later, take the time to access your feelings.

2. Accept these emotions for what they are

It's easy to read information and nod as it all makes sense. Unfortunately, it's not so easy to remember it when faced with specific challenges. When your blood is boiling, or you feel like there are enough tears to compete with Niagara Falls, it's hard to tell yourself that these emotions have a purpose.

A good affirmation that can be used to calm yourself down or to begin working through your feelings is, "My emotions are trying to tell me something." It's not always obvious. Sometimes, you have to peel back a few layers before it becomes clear, much like an onion. Nevertheless, this affirmation allows us to put some distance between our raw emotions and our logical selves to get to the roots of what we are feeling.

3. Assess the cause of the emotions

Again, there will be days when this is simple and other days when it is less so. Are you stressed about other things in your life, and has this caused stronger emotions than usual or perhaps unwarranted ones?

For example, if you are having a tight month financially and your mobile bill is $30 more, the feeling of despair will be higher than at a time when your finances aren't an issue.

Also, things like tiredness and hunger will exacerbate any situation. On the other hand, eating a healthy meal, getting a good night's sleep, or even just resting can shine a new light on a problem.

Depending on the emotion, you may also consider

whether you are at fault in a particular situation. If your kids tell you they hate you—what caused their outburst? Just because you are an adult doesn't mean you are always right. They are also still learning about their emotional management and need to learn from your example.

Recognize that sometimes our feelings are unjustified. Looking at another previous example, if a partner cheats on you, you have the right to feel angry and devastated. But you are not weak, nor are you inferior or a bad person. Your partner has chosen to act in this way. Their actions are their responsibility. How you act is yours.

4. Journal your emotions for further clarity

Think of your emotions like your shopping list. A mental shopping list is almost OK, but you are likely to forget at least one thing with so much going on in your mind.

Writing about our experiences and emotions gives us a clearer view. It's amazing how after a short time writing, you can go back and reread your words only to have things make so much more sense.

It also gives you the necessary time to process all of your emotions. You write about something more often than not, and it reminds you of something else that you need to get off your chest. If we leave all of this bouncing around in our brains, it's difficult to organize our thoughts.

5. Play out different scenarios in your mind or journal

By now, you should be feeling calmer, and the logical part of your brain helps make sense of things.

Now is the time to look at the outcome you want. How can you resolve the situation or problem so that your emotions and the emotions of others are taken care of?

It is wise to treat this step as you would any other problem—brainstorm to solve the problem in at least two or three ways. Then, look at the pros and cons for each and decide on the best solution.

You can take this a step further and look at the potential emotions you will feel based on each given outcome. This is not to say that you are a fortune-teller or mind-reader.

But preparing yourself for possible emotions will help you keep them under control and therefore not react negatively.

These five steps should become part of a routine. It will require more effort at first but gets easier and quicker each time you practice. The more control you get over the initial emotion, the less likely you will react so quickly.

With this, you have a greater ability to see situations for what they are and appreciate the advice your emotions are trying to give you.

Managing emotions throughout difficult conversations

You would think that as we get older, it would be easier to have difficult conversations without our emotions getting the better of us. There might be certain relationships where this is true, for example, your parents or a long-term partner.

But even then, a new situation arises and communication stalls. There is a greater probability of the conversation going smoothly if at least one of you can leave emotions out of the equation. That's not to say that you shouldn't make your feelings clear.

• Always prepare what you want to say. For example, use "I" statements to focus on how you feel rather than attacking another person's behavior.

• Choose the right time to have the conversation. It is best to do so when you are calm. For example, if the person you plan to talk to has just walked in the door, or you know they are tired or hungry, wait until they have had a chance to relax.

• Focus on your body language. Arms and legs crossed can come across as defensive. Shoulders hunched may appear passive. Hands behind your back imply you are hiding something. Try to keep your frame open and make eye contact.

• Be specific about your emotions. Bearing in mind how

complex they are, the other person may need more than "I feel angry" or "I feel sad." Again, you can label your emotions accurately in the planning phase.

- Actively listen to what they have to say. You can't respond appropriately if you only take in what you want to hear. Make a conscious effort not to interrupt. Use a timer if one or both of you are prone to interrupting.

- Be careful of "hooks". These are phrases that a person will use to either manipulate you or cause a particular reaction. Don't forget that they will be hoping for a reaction. Pause and take a deep breath before responding.

If there comes the point during these challenging conversations where you aren't getting anywhere, or you can feel that your emotions are becoming harder to control, take a step away—a time out.

Let the other person know that you want to talk, but you need a few minutes to center yourself.

The importance of using the right language

There are two areas that I would like to just touch on at this point—using negative words and changing your perspective.

When we looked at the complexity of our emotions, we began by listing as many emotions as possible and then deciding which were positive and negative. We put this down to negativity bias. However, there is another reason.

The emotions that lead to negative consequences take more effort to process. Think about words like disgust, hatred, fright, and so on. It leads to the next question, why? The answer includes complex explanations and emotions.

Compare this to the word happy or even surprise. If you feel happy or someone else tells you they are happy, you don't question its reason.

Fifty per cent of the words we use are negative, regardless of age or culture. Conversely, thirty percent are positive, and twenty percent are neutral (Schrauf, 2005).

We can relate this to managing our emotions because if we can't pinpoint and label the emotion straight away, we will spend more time and effort searching through 'negative words' until we get the right one.

On the other hand, during a difficult conversation, if we have assessed how we are feeling and correctly labeled this emotion, we won't list various other negative emotions before letting the other person know how we feel.

Secondly, and this too relates to our planning stage, we can look at the benefits of a change in perspective.

Changing your mindset refers to yourself in the third person rather than the first person.

You may indeed have seen a movie or series character, or even a friend who refers to themselves in the third person and thought them to be a bit crazy. However, using your own name instead of "I" has been proven to increase people's ability to control thoughts, feelings, and behavior in stressful situations.

How is this achieved? Using third-person pronouns such as he or she as well as your name creates distance between yourself and the situation (Kross et al., 2014). This distance enables you to see things from a different perspective.

It's the same principle as giving advice to a friend. It's always easier to look at things objectively when it's not your problem. This provides you with the opportunity to offer potential solutions that your friend may not have thought of.

So when it comes to choosing the correct language to help manage difficult emotions, not only should we be careful about negative words (including words like not, never, nobody, etc.), but it is also worth trying to refer to yourself by your own name.

Put it into practice

Aside from the steps discussed above, other constructive techniques can help you overcome feelings of negativity.

Let's start with some simple methods. Once you start seeing the positive impact, you can work on those that might be more challenging.

- **Symbolic release**—write down your emotions on strips of paper. Light a fire and throw each strip into the fire.

- **Get creative**—if you aren't a writer, draw your emotions or make a collage from magazine images.

- **Create a playlist**—don't just make a playlist of happy songs; this is like the musical version of toxic positivity. Include pieces that represent how you feel at the time.

- **Be your own agony aunt/uncle**—write a short message describing your situation and feelings. Respond to your name so that you are creating distance and widening perspectives.

- **Find your emotional outlet**—imagine you have an emotion tap. Whether it's exercise, laughing at YouTube videos, or hanging out with friends, imagine this tap opens and helps to drain away any potential harmful build-up.

- **Start disregarding those who create negativity**—the energy vampires, the "Eeyores" of the world, the toxic manipulators, etc. If you can't ignore them, at least create distance. All these people will undo all the fantastic work you are doing.

With correct emotional management, you won't suddenly notice that negative feelings disappear—they are vital. What happens is that we accept this moment and know that at this particular time, as you process how you feel, it's OK not to be OK because this time will pass.

> *"Mourning, as we know, however painful it may be, comes to a spontaneous end. When it has renounced everything that has been lost, then it has consumed itself, and our libido is once more free to replace the lost objects by fresh ones equally or still more precious."*
>
> — SIGMUND FREUD

Remember to be patient with yourself. The spontaneous end to your feelings might come tomorrow or next week. As long as you know that you are doing everything you can to work through your feelings, it will come.

Now that you are well on your way to emotional management, it's time to look at how we can achieve similar success with our thoughts.

CHAPTER 7: HOW TO CONTROL YOUR THOUGHTS FOR OPTIMISTIC OUTCOMES

When was the last time you were stuck in a thought loop and were unable to stop this obsessive thinking?

Perhaps it was something you started thinking about last week, and it is still burning a hole in your mind. Maybe it's a daily occurrence? While these moments often include negative thinking, sometimes, it is just overthinking a decision or a situation that has happened or might happen.

Negative thinking is exhausting, but overthinking can be just as draining on your physical and mental self. Again, let's use a family event as an example.

So many of us haven't been able to see our families for months, maybe even years now. Despite COVID-19 still being an issue, there are fewer restrictions, so travel is now possible. Here is what overthinking looks like:

- I'm so desperate to see all of my family and have an excellent non-virtual get-together, but…

- Granny is getting older, and what if I unknowingly give her COVID-19, but…

- Mom hasn't seen the kids in ages, but…

- What about the cost of tests and all the paperwork but…

- I've been working so hard, and I need this break, but…

- I can't afford to get COVID-19 and then be stuck in a hotel quarantine, but…

- I've been vaccinated; it should be safe…and so on!

If you haven't thought of five more "buts", you will probably go back to the first. Notice that there are some negatives, some fears, some excitement, and clearly some mixed emotions.

A quick mini-practice here: identify something you have been ruminating about recently. Have a quick brain dump of all the ands and buts that are part of these thoughts

Overthinking doesn't just happen with the bigger things in life. Here is a list of the top ten things people tend to overthink:

1. How to get out of a plan

2. What to wear for a particular occasion

3. Financial choices like saving or investing

4. Whether their attempted banter at work offended someone

5. How to ask someone to pay back money owing to them

6. The wording of a text message received

7. Why a specific person hasn't immediately responded to a text

8. What friends think of us

9. How much to spend on a gift

10. Why a friend never called back

In a 2003 study by Henry Holt and Company, fifty-two percent of 45-year-olds overthink. For 25–35-year-olds, the percentage is higher at seventy-three percent. Overthinking a response to a text message takes an average of nine minutes (Kool Mornings Radio, 2020).

Overthinking often leads to analysis paralysis, a concept whereby we think so much, it prevents us from making any decision. Options go around the brain, but as no decision is made, no action is taken, and we never know if a choice is right or wrong.

There are physical implications to overthinking too. We have less energy, and some people struggle to sleep.

Overthinking impacts our appetite; some people turn to stress-eating, while others can't face the thought of food.

Studies have also shown that overthinking reduces our creativity. For example, sixteen women and fourteen men underwent MRI scans while drawing different pictures. Some were simple, others more complex. The drawings were captured in specially designed MRI-safe electronic tablets.

After analyzing the drawings, researchers found that the more complex the pictures, the less creativity was used (Stanford Medicine, 2015).

The irony here is that we need as much creativity as possible in problem-solving. But, unfortunately, the more we think about a problem, the harder it becomes to solve.

Controlling negative thoughts and reducing overthinking will lead to a quieter mind. But, more than that, it will allow you to be more confident in your decision-making, whether it's responding to a text or buying a new house.

There are various tools to help you become the master of your thoughts—we will start with the popular choice of mindfulness.

What is the mindfulness tool RAIN?

For those keen to be more in the present, we have seen how mindful practices can help. Indeed, mindfulness isn't a tool for everyone, particularly those with an open mind.

It may require practice before you begin to see the benefits.

With this in mind, we will look at RAIN, a mindfulness tool developed by Michelle McDonald. I like RAIN because it provides a simple framework that allows us to deal with difficult emotions without judging ourselves and flitting between the past and the future.

RAIN is an acronym for Recognize, Accept, Investigate, and Not-Identify. Some steps will seem familiar, but it does help to use RAIN to stay on track.

1. Recognize

Yes, it all begins with recognizing the thoughts going through your mind. Then, take a step back and understand the ideas that open the door to accurately defining the emotion.

Neither the thought nor the emotion should be judged. So if, for example, the idea of going to your room and closing yourself off from the family dramatics comes to mind, don't judge yourself and tell yourself you're a terrible person.

2. Accept

The key to accepting or allowing this feeling is not trying to change it. You might not like the thought that's in your mind, but as with emotions, if you try not to think about it, it only becomes more potent. So say your thought out loud without adding how you feel.

When we add emotions to thoughts, they become difficult to accept.

For example, my thought is to lock myself in a quiet place. If I add a feeling, it becomes complex; I feel guilty for thinking about locking myself in a calm area. You then have to accept the thought and emotion!

3. Investigate

You can combine your investigation with third-person distancing.

For example, create a dialogue between yourself as Holmes and your third person as Sherlock. Remember that it's a friendly investigation, not a session on the couch with Freud.

Ask questions like, when did this thought first appear? Is this a new thought, or is it recurring? Are there people or situations that spark this thought?

4. You are not your emotions

You are not your thoughts or your emotions. You are a complete entity that experiences thoughts and feelings. Thoughts are frequently caused by outside forces that come and go.

When you can identify yourself as separate from the thought, you see yourself as a whole person, not restricted or limited. It keeps you in the present as you recognize this is just a moment.

Put it into practice

Imagine you are scrolling through your social media. Your brain is one of your friends and often posts thoughts online. For example, as you scroll through your feed, you read, "Brain posted a comment- I don't want to go to that party."

You read the post, ask why Brain doesn't want to go to the party and what happened. Then, keep scrolling. This simple visualization tool incorporates all the RAIN frameworks in a way that we are accustomed to—scrolling through social media.

Of course, there will never be a single solution to overcome negativity and overthinking. Even psychologists will have differing opinions. For this reason, we will now look at how we can reframe our thought patterns and essentially change the way we think.

How to reframe negative thinking and reduce overthinking?

Reframing negative thoughts is a process used in Cognitive Behavioral Therapy (CBT) to turn negative interpretations into more positive ones.

Before reframing negative thoughts and negative thought patterns, we need a better understanding of the type of thoughts we have. According to psychiatrist David Burns, who based his work on Aaron Beck's 1976 theory, fifteen common cognitive distortions influence our thinking.

1. Filtering—despite being presented with positives and negatives, we filter the positive and only listen to the negative.

2. Polarization—seeing things at polar extremes, like only black or white. This leads to high standards and a greater chance of failing.

3. Overgeneralization—when something doesn't go our way, and we use words like always, never, and everything. For example, "I always mess up everything."

4. Discounting the positive—when someone pays us a compliment, and we dismiss it. Perhaps we think they are just saying it to be nice.

5. Jumping to conclusions—we believe something when we have no evidence. For example, if our partner seems distant, we assume they must be having an affair rather than having a bad day.

6. Catastrophizing—not only do we jump to the wrong conclusion, but we also blow it entirely out of proportion. For example, the boss calls you in, and you immediately assume you're getting fired.

7. Personalization—we take responsibility for everything, even when the circumstances are out of our control. However, we can also be overly sensitive regarding our own beliefs. For example, if someone is talking about their religion or political views, we might take it as a criticism of our own.

8. Control fallacies—the need to control everyone and everything, or the opposite extreme of feeling completely out of control.

9. The fallacy of fairness—each person has their own idea of fairness and what we see as fair is often in our favor. Dealing with people who don't see fairness in the same way can lead to confrontation and resentment.

10. Blaming—it's not just about making others responsible for how we feel. It's a dangerous cognitive distortion because we believe that those we blame can affect or even control our lives.

11. "Shoulds"—shoulds like "I should be feeling better" create rules in our lives that leave little room for compromise. There is pressure to fulfil expectations. It does not allow for changes in circumstances that are beyond our control.

12. Emotional reasoning—your feelings tend to dictate what you think is reality. If you feel a niggling anxious feeling on waking, it's a sign of a bad day. There is no distinction between feeling and facts.

13. The fallacy of chance—expecting other people to change. They will come around to your way of thinking with enough pressure, and your needs will be met.

14. Global labeling—is an extreme form of overgeneralization whereby you judge yourself or others

based on just one event. For example, you see a well-dressed woman in designer clothes and label them high maintenance.

15. Always being right—many of us have a desire to be right at times. However, it becomes a cognitive distortion when you go to great lengths to prove this.

(The Feeling Good Handbook, Burns, 1989)

With quite an extensive list, you may need a little time to become confident at understanding which of the categories your thoughts fall into. Take your time because there are different strategies to reframe negative thoughts, and some work better on particular categories and vice-versa.

Here are three ways to start reframing your thoughts for more positive outcomes.

The immediate stop

This is one of the quickest ways to stop a negative thought from progressing. As soon as a negative thought comes into your mind, you tell yourself to stop. You can say it out loud or, if there are people around, you might want to imagine a huge stop sign in front of you.

Correct your negative thought at once. Don't replace it with a toxic positive but rather with a truth. Here's how it works:

You are feeling extremely nervous about a meeting or presentation. The negative thought "I can't do this" invades your mind.

"STOP! I'm nervous, but I can do this, and I'm going to learn and grow from the experience."

It's a little bit like an arm wrestle. The negative thought may try to overpower your "Stop" sentence. In this case, you need to repeat the sentence with more force and conviction on certain words like "can" and "going to." Visualize this arm wrestle and your sentence overpowering the negative thought.

Rephrase negative thoughts

For every negative phrase you come up with, take a few minutes to write down or think about three opposites. For example:

This evening is going to be a disaster

1. This evening, I get to see X, whom I haven't seen for a while.

2. This evening, I can have some adult time with my partner.

3. This evening, I get to try the new restaurant I have wanted to visit.

Journal about your negative thoughts

Start by recognizing your negative thoughts and deciding if there is any truth behind them. Is there evidence to prove or disprove your opinions? Next, ask yourself what has happened for these thoughts to occur and how you can approach the same thoughts from different angles, much like rephrasing it.

Also, think if these thoughts have served you in any way. Often, the lesson that we learn is not to jump to conclusions or make assumptions. We can learn that our negative self-talk is often unjustified too. From what you have learned, decide if you can handle thoughts and situations or people who lead to these thoughts differently.

Put it into practice

Putting a stop to negative thinking and overthinking requires overcoming negative self-talk. If I asked you right now to list your strengths, it might take a minute or even more. The longer it takes to remember our strengths, the more time negative thoughts have to develop.

Create a list of your strengths; leave space at the end to continue adding to the list. Then, for inspiration, think about some of these strengths:

- Appreciative
- Artistic

- Athletic
- Clever
- Curious
- Detail-oriented
- Energetic
- Flexible
- Focused
- Helpful
- Humble
- Inspirational
- Logical
- Organized
- Respectful
- Responsible
- Straightforward
- Trustworthy
- Warm

Many times, it helps us to see the bigger picture. However, with negative thoughts, the bigger picture might be too overwhelming. Break the negative into smaller chunks.

Finally, attach one of your strengths to each chunk of negativity. Focus on this strength as it will help you work through the negative. This will help you to develop a strategy to overcome negative thoughts.

Mind hacking quick-fix trick to control overthinking and anxiety

When you start ruminating, feeling anxious, or experiencing overwhelming negative thoughts, try this simple practice to retain control, stay calm, and feel comfortable in just a few minutes.

1. Sit down. Immerse yourself in the sensations of your body and your inner state.

2. Allow yourself to feel any unpleasant sensations or discomfort.

3. Stay like this for a few minutes and feel the discomfort.

Shift your attention to the part of your body that feels most comfortable. It could be anything—your ear, stomach, pinky finger, etc. Experience this sense of comfort for a few minutes. Let this feeling expand all over your body, and you will feel much better. Your mood will improve.

4. Repeat several times.

As hard as this sounds, even when we get better control of our emotions and thoughts, we will still come up against situations that will be upsetting, frustrating, draining, and so on. In the next chapter, we will look at ways to help make these situations easier to handle and even more enjoyable.

CHAPTER 8: GETTING THROUGH THOSE CHALLENGING EXPERIENCES WITH A LITTLE LESS MISERY

Imagine that everything in life is going your way. You are walking with your head that little bit higher, and all of the efforts you have made so far are paying off.

Then you get to work and learn your next project involves working with your least favorite colleague. Or your children have failed their exams and need a tutor.

Even during our most joyous moments, something can happen that pulls us back down to square one—or at least that's how it feels.

There are ways to handle these situations, so you don't fall back into negative thinking or suppress these feelings with toxic positivity.

We will work through some of these challenging situations so you remain on the right track.

How to get "unstuck" and move on from a difficult experience

This is a personal favorite of mine—that moment when you are stuck in a rut and aren't sure which side of the track to start digging. The feeling of being stuck can occur when faced with challenges but can also appear spontaneously.

You might have a birthday is coming up, and you feel like you aren't going anywhere in life. Or you may have reached a goal and aren't sure what's next.

Here are some suggestions to try when you have exhausted other techniques. You have attempted to solve a problem in many ways and have assessed and reassessed your goals, making adjustments when necessary. But, if you still can't shake the feeling of being stuck, here is an out-of-the-box idea that could revolutionize your thinking.

Consider that you are in this rut, but instead of not knowing which side to dig, you are scared to make the right move. This implies that you know the solution to becoming unstuck, but your fear prevents you from taking action.

We also know at this stage that our fear is telling us something. So, again, before we start digging, we will calm our parasympathetic nervous system, analyze this fear, and decide if it is warranted. If it is justified, then the answer is incorrect.

If the fear is unwarranted, then it needs to be overcome. But, when someone tells us to grab the bull by the horns and get on with it, it's about as much use as a toxic positivity statement.

It would help if you had the confidence to overcome fear. Without experience, you struggle to find become confident. But still, fear is stopping you from gaining confidence. So take the challenge out of the equation and look for alternative ways to overcome fear and become more confident.

Let's take public speaking as an example. You have been asked to speak in public in a month, on a stage and with a digital presentation. Of course, this challenge exposes all kinds of negative feelings, assumptions, and fears. But most of all, you are telling yourself you can't do it. So rather than trying to overcome this massive fear, you can work on more minor unrelated fears to build confidence.

Take a completely different fear—maybe it's a fear of heights, a fear of failing a recipe, or not passing an exam. Start with a slight worry, for example, the recipe. Then, when no one is watching, prepare the recipe. If it doesn't work, do it again and again until it's perfect. Finally, cook for your family, and the fear has gone. Instead, your confidence is enhanced.

Then repeat with the next fear until you are confident, and so on. How is this related to getting yourself out of a rut? Each fear you overcome gives you a chance to rephrase the negative.

Instead of "I can't do it", you rephrase the negative by saying, "I thought I couldn't do it, but I did it when I made that recipe." Each win builds your confidence and helps you overcome your fears. With enough practice, your conscious and subconscious develop experience in overcoming fears. The fear keeping you in the rut will no longer be a hurdle; it will just be the next fear to overcome.

It won't be long before you appreciate the personal growth that is allowing you to overcome a specific challenge as well as the challenges life throws at you.

Make sure to respond to negative situations in the right way

This one is a bit more difficult because there is a considerable spectrum of adverse conditions. For example, not finding a job or a family member is causing conflict.

Don't delay dealing with adverse situations. Negative situations rarely resolve themselves. Plus, the longer it takes to react, the more chance the problem will grow.

It doesn't matter what negative situation you are facing—always start in the right frame of mind. For example, use the deep breathing method, splash water on your face, or practice mindfulness for a few minutes to bring yourself back to the present.

Check in with your negative thoughts and emotions. The difference between getting past a negative situation and becoming stuck in a negative loop will lie in your ability to accept and reframe these thoughts and feelings.

Always accept responsibility in adverse situations. That's not to say that the cause or the result is your fault. But you are responsible for the way you respond. The trick here is that if you hold on to your negatives, you won't take responsibility—the brain can't do it!

Taking responsibility doesn't sound like much, but it is a massive step towards taking control of your situation. Automatic responses are not a sign that we are in control.

Process your emotions and thoughts as discussed in the previous chapters, and tell yourself that you will not make decisions based on negative feelings. You will be able to respond to negative situations appropriately.

Learning lessons from our mistakes

We fear getting things wrong! The negative self-talk that comes with making mistakes blocks any potential learning. Those who think they can get through life without falling short will never live up to their true potential.

We make mistakes when we try new things, step out of

our comfort zone, or explore solutions to problems. However, just because a mistake was made once doesn't mean it will happen again; that's just lousy fortune-telling.

Every mistake we make becomes a lesson. Some are obvious—the hangover after too many drinks the previous night or accusing someone of something without having the facts. Other mistakes need closer inspection to learn from them.

Not only do we have to take responsibility for our mistakes, but we also need to say the words out loud and to those who need to hear them. For example, saying "It's a shame it didn't work out" is not the same as "I messed up."

Set a time limit. The amount of time will depend on the severity of the mistake. But if we don't put a time limit to learn from our mistakes, we will find ourselves dwelling on the error for longer than necessary.

We must reflect on and take responsibility for our mistakes. We must look at what led to the errors and ask what might have happened had we done something differently. What outcomes could we expect by changing specific actions?

Next is to write a list of why we don't want to make the same mistake again. Again, this is not done to reflect on the adverse outcomes. Instead, it's a reminder to keep us on track and remain self-disciplined.

For example, if we have run up debt on our credit cards, we should include what will happen if we repeat the same mistake. Likewise, if we want to eliminate a particular toxic person from our life, we should talk about what will happen if we let them manipulate us again?

The final step is to make a plan that is strict but allows for flexibility. Most importantly, the strategy must include measures to prevent us from making the same mistake again, based on what we have learned.

Using objective reality to solve problems

I'm no philosopher, but we need to get our head around the concept of objective reality before using it to solve problems. Remember that objective and subjective realities are up for much debate, so we can freely form our own opinions.

Objective reality is the belief that things exist independent of the mind. Subjective reality is the perceived reality of the mind. Here are some examples in a somewhat simplified form.

A flower is a flower, and we know that it exists, but we can't know of its existence without looking at it, touching it, or smelling it. So it's subjective. Each person may have a different opinion on this flower. On the other hand, objective reality argues that, for example, the Statue of Liberty exists in New York. This is universally accepted, and there is no room for subjective interpretations.

Before getting lost in a world of quantum physics and parallel universes, we should look at how objective reality can help us through difficult times.

To be objective is much like objective reality. Take any problem, and we know that it exists. If we let subjectivity in, we essentially make the situation worse because our mind influences it.

To be objective, we must be impartial, fair, and open-minded. There is no bias or emotions, just neutrality. It's our emotions that take control. As soon as we remove emotions, we are no longer emotionally invested. Of course, we still can't afford to ignore our feelings, but we can choose to put them to one side.

One way to become more objective is to stop running on autopilot. We have probably been hit with challenge after challenge for a long time and have automatically put our head down and gotten on with it. After all, we're too busy to sit down and change what has apparently worked until now.

Unfortunately, this fixed mindset makes it extremely difficult to change our behavior and find a better way of facing challenges. A fixed mindset limits our beliefs and, more specifically, the belief in our potential.

Trying new experiences opens the mind. Instead of using the same go-to method to address a task, find new, more efficient ways. New experiences introduce us to more people, cultures, values, each one readjusting biases that we might have.

One tip for objectivity is to take a business approach. For example, managers and business owners use cost-benefit analysis for decision-making. This is a systematic approach to understanding strengths and weaknesses.

This is easier in business as you can put numbers to the costs and the benefits. But to face a challenge objectively, you can still create a list of the benefits and costs to evaluate the most favorable outcome.

For objectivity to work, I strongly advise you to take a breath first and process those thoughts and emotions, even if it's just five minutes of journaling. It's tough to put your feelings to one side if they are still niggling away at you.

Some people are highly unrealistic about the reality they live in. They refuse to accept that bad things happen and that suffering exists. For this, an understanding of tragic optimism is necessary.

What is tragic optimism?

What does the antidote to toxic positivity look like? Tragic optimism! Victor Frankl, professor and holocaust survivor, was the first to coin the term tragic optimism—it is a way of living in the face of adversity. He put forward to 'tragic triad':

1. Pain and suffering

2. Guilt because we make our own choices and take responsibility for those choices

3. Death, and knowing that our life is transient

(The Case for Tragic Optimism, Frankl, 1984)

Frankl believed that it was necessary to learn from the tragic triad to find meaning in life. People can then find true happiness. Nobody can begin to imagine the pain and suffering Frankl went through during his three years in a concentration camp, the death he saw, and the guilt he felt for surviving.

It has been shown that different people will grow in different ways after experiencing tragedy. For example, post-traumatic growth may include a deeper appreciation for life or gratitude for relationships. In addition, some people are more compassionate, they have a better sense of their abilities, and others find a greater purpose.

Ch-19 has to be the most relevant example of tragic optimism. There is no way we can be grateful for the pandemic, and everyone has been touched by it one way or another. But it has changed the way most people view the world and their lives.

In a 2020 study, fifty-six percent of people felt more grateful during the first terrifying months of the pandemic. These people also felt happier (Watkins et al., 2021).

There is a difference between being grateful and telling

ourselves things could always be worse. We can look at the pandemic and think that things could be worse, but this isn't accepting the pain. Instead, you tell yourself that you don't have the right to be angry or upset.

Instead, we can use phrases like:

- Even though times are hard, I am grateful for my life

- Through suffering, I have been able to learn the importance of gratitude

- This has been a tough time, but I am thankful that I'm still here

- Some of the people in my life may test me, but I am grateful they are still around

- I am thankful for this challenge because I can learn and grow from it

In each of the above phrases, we do not pretend that pain and suffering don't exist. On the contrary, we accept it and recognize that some good can derive from it.

How to respond to bad news

Like challenges and mistakes, it's unlikely that we will go through life without some bad news. This isn't being negative—just realistic. Learning how to handle bad news will help us deal with the emotions and thoughts that follow.

Before looking at how to deal with bad news, I felt it is

essential to turn some attention to those who deliver it. The way news is imparted can affect our response; the person might appear unsympathetic, even cold. But it is also true that one can't control others.

Remember the following things about people who deliver bad news:

- They are never going to be happy about your bad news

- They want to say the right thing but don't know how

- It's hard for people not to think about themselves when delivering bad news

- People don't intentionally make things worse

- If they use toxic positivity, it's because they genuinely believe it will help

It might surprise you to know that stress and anxiety help us to process bad news (The Journal of Neuroscience, 2018). This is another example of how amazingly tuned the body is to dealing with negativity and using the information received to react accordingly.

The type of bad news is going to affect your response. For example, if you have just been told you have lost your job—you feel panicked. So much is rushing through your mind: how you will find a new job? How are you going to pay the bills?

Nevertheless, if you allow this to remain the center of focus, you will miss out on a learning opportunity, and that is feedback. Reacting with anger or aggression will only encourage the other person to end the situation. Begging for a second chance or promising to do better is probably too little too late, and it might not even be the reason for the dismissal.

The time to process thoughts and emotions is later, when you are at home. Make the most of this challenging situation by asking what you can do to improve. The feedback you are given provides an opportunity for growth.

More devastating news like loss or the death of a loved one is never easy to process, so don't underestimate your emotions.

In these cases, the first thing is to focus on your health. Terrible news can lead to hyperventilation, dizziness, and panic attacks. Sit down and breathe. It's impossible to know how you will respond in these situations. You might feel anger, relief, a sense of emptiness, but just for a few minutes, breathe, and don't let the initial wave of emotions cause negative consequences.

With loss and grief, we often need to take care of others. If your father dies, you need to be there for your mother. If your partner leaves, the children have to come first. There is no way around this.

However, don't fall into the trap of constantly putting other people first. Time will pass, and you will have suppressed your emotions instead of grieving.

There may come a moment when all the people who depend on you are asleep, and all you want to do is go to bed and sleep too. Instead, take this quiet time and do whatever you need to let those difficult emotions out. Cry, sing, dance, scream, journal, look through photo albums.

There is no single answer for everyone—except that you have to make time for yourself.

Put it into practice:

Because we have concentrated on emotions and thought patterns, this practice is related to objectivity. So, as we work through our feelings, we can now think of more objectively of solutions.

One technique that will help is S.W.O.T.:

- **S**trengths—what are your strengths? What internal resources are available to help you; what positive attributes do you possess that would offer you a competitive advantage?

- **W**eaknesses—what are your weaknesses? What factors place you at a disadvantage? How can you prepare for the challenges ahead?

- **O**pportunities—what opportunities are open to you that would improve your skills, for example, courses or TED talks; see opportunities as chances for something positive to happen.

- **T**hreats—what threats could impact your efforts; these

could include external factors or internal weaknesses. Challenges are often like buses. You might go through months or even a year or so without anything out of the ordinary happening. Then all of a sudden, three or four giant obstacles all come your way.

It's not bad luck, and you haven't done anything to deserve this. However, it would help if you didn't fool yourself into thinking that you have had your fair share of bad luck and that life will only get better. It is what it is.

If you fear these challenges, you will stop living life to the full. But, on the other hand, if you try to prepare for or prevent all obstacles, you will also spend more time in the future and miss out on the present.

The best way to get through the significant challenges in life is to work on your emotional and thought management continuously. And tackle the more minor obstacles so that you build the confidence to tackle the more significant challenges when they arise.

The last challenge that we will cover is toxic positivity from others. Now that you are aware of its dangers, you will see how frequently people use it. But, unfortunately, not everyone has your newfound knowledge, so we must learn to handle various situations where people tell us how we should be feeling.

CHAPTER 9: HOW TO DEAL WITH TOXIC POSITIVITY FROM OTHERS

In my case, after understanding toxic positivity and the harm it could do, I started to see it everywhere. I would talk to a friend, and the best I would get was, "Everything will be alright in the end." I had previously used social media as my go-to for a break and recharge. Now, I saw that my family and friends' posts consisted only of positive vibe memes.

You might want to shout out, "Can't you see what this is doing to you?" but they haven't had the same opportunity as you to recognize what toxic positivity is. Unfortunately, some people have no idea, and others will use toxic positivity to get what they want from you. This last chapter will focus on techniques to protect ourselves from toxic positivity.

How to respond to toxic positivity

This is a challenge in itself. It is easy to identify toxic

positivity, but if you aren't careful with your response, some might think you are negative or call you out. Nevertheless, if you don't explain why you aren't going down the positive vibes only road, they won't stop.

Unintentionally, these people are trying to control your feelings. But, unfortunately, the effort you have put into doing this yourself can't be undone.

Don't be angry when someone offers you a toxic positivity affirmation to help you. You can feel angry and frustrated, but it would be inappropriate to be angry. This isn't emotional management.

We often assume that the person offering us toxic advice isn't strong enough to cope with our emotions. This is a cognitive distortion as we are making assumptions or mind-reading! As long as we aren't projecting negativity onto others, it's OK to talk about how we feel.

It's also hard to tell someone they are wrong, especially if we aren't in the best frame of mind. So there is no need to make a big deal out of it. Instead, we need to take a moment to assess how the comment makes us feel.

There will be a brief pause in the conversation. They might be feeling uncomfortable about our problems or challenges. But, on the other hand, it's possible they are lost for words and filling the silence.

Rather than go into the details of toxic positivity, tell them what you would like from them. Perhaps you just want to vent, or you need someone to bounce ideas off. They don't know unless you tell them.

Here are some useful phrases that you can use to respond to toxic positivity:

- I don't need advice. I just need someone who will listen.

- If I go through what is bothering me, can you just check to see if it all sounds reasonable?

- When you recognize my feelings, it's easier for me to process them.

- How I feel right now is only temporary.

- Not all of my experiences are positive; some are even quite painful.

- Right now, I'm grieving, and this is going to help me move forward.

- It's OK not to be OK some of the time.

- I am grateful, but that doesn't mean I am not also in pain.

Often, these phrases provide a tremendous amount of relief for the person. They suddenly have direction, and they know what to do. That's not to say that the behavior will stop for good. If you notice a pattern where someone relies on toxic positivity, you may need to talk to them.

Be careful, though. Essentially, you are advising someone

on how to give advice. If that isn't enough, you are informing them that their positive vibes may actually be having the opposite effect. Before pointing this out to people, ask them if they are open to feedback or have heard about toxic positivity.

What can you do when others project toxic positivity?

When people are constantly trying to project toxic positivity onto you, it's time for you to put your empathy skills to good use. Telling themselves or you that everything will be OK and that there is always a silver lining is a way to reinforce their own toxic positivity.

Little do they know is that their bubble is made of glass and can smash at any moment.

If you have already responded to a person's toxic positivity and they don't seem to have understood the point you are trying to make, you need to ask what is causing them to rely on it so much.

There is a strong likelihood that you are more aware of your thoughts and feelings than others. Ask yourself what might be happening in their life that is causing them to repeat the affirmation, "Just be happy."

The next time you notice them trying to push toxic positivity, don't tell them what might be going on. Instead, ask them if they would like to talk. Then, find time to get rid of distractions and sit down and listen.

With your newfound knowledge, you might want to share your advice on toxic positivity; tell them they should accept their emotions for what they are.

Listen carefully to what they say and only offer advice when they ask for it. Don't judge and don't react to their emotions.

Of course, sometimes you can correctly respond to toxic positivity and be there for those constantly projecting this positivity. In this case, you might be dealing with a narcissist.

Preventing narcissists using toxic positivity to control you

Narcissists can be extremely dangerous, but the relationship can reach a whole new level of darkness when you add toxic positivity. Before looking at how narcissists use toxic positivity, consider this.

You may have been using toxic positivity to cover your issues with a narcissist. For example, you might tell yourself that things aren't as bad as they seem or that, deep down, they love you and that you are lucky to have them in your life.

This doesn't just apply to partners; it can be any relationship. It is unhealthy to bury the feelings caused by a narcissist, and you deserve to have relationships where you are free to express how you feel.

Even though you have been working to remove the toxic

positivity from your life, it's also possible that this is the last area that you need to tackle because it is the most difficult.

Nevertheless, with all the strategies you have discussed so far, you will be able to plan a conversation that enables you to manage your emotions. Narcissists love with an idealized grandiose image of themselves.

Narcissists live in a fantasy bubble. In their world, everything is great, and they like to make sure that those in their lives feel the same. So they will be offended if you have a bad day and potentially bring that negativity into their life.

Their behavior is self-centered and arrogant. If a narcissist asks you how your day was or how you are, they expect you to mirror their positivity and say that everything is great. It's almost as if you don't have the right to express any negative feelings because this is reserved for them. After all, they are more important.

If you try to talk about a problem you are having or let them know that you are feeling low, they will turn this back on you. It will be your own fault because you don't have a positive attitude.

Common narcissistic comments include "Why are you always in such a bad mood?" or "Why can't you just be happy." Narcissists lack empathy; they are unaware of or don't care about your emotions.

This is a form of extreme gaslighting. This person will eventually lead you to question your own mind. You will start to feel like you are a negative person, too sensitive or emotional.

Before attempting any discussion with a manipulator, consider whether there is any truth to what they are saying. For example, if they accuse you of being negative all the time, it might be that you are negative only when you are with them.

Narcissists' relationships are one-sided. They must be reminded that you too have feelings, thoughts, values, and beliefs to be respected if the relationship is to survive.

It's also important to share your expectations with a narcissist. For example, if you are dealing with a colleague, you need to let them know in advance that the task requires cooperation and that reward or credit is to be shared.

It helps to set consequences with narcissists. For example, if you can't express your feelings, you won't spend time with them. It sounds harsh, but this approach is often the only way a narcissist will learn that their behavior is unacceptable.

If there comes the point where no conversation is going to stop a narcissist from using toxic positivity, you have to consider whether it is time to end the relationship.

It's very rare for a narcissist to change, despite their promises. Use the cost-benefit approach or the S.W.O.T. method to make an objective decision.

Get good at talking about toxic positivity with your "infected" friends

Toxic positivity shouldn't be a taboo subject. It is a topic that should be spoken about because it can be harmful to one's health and well-being. It invalidates people's feelings and emotions. Speaking about toxic positivity will help promote negative emotions as natural and normal.

There are specific topics that we would consider negative. However, if friends talk about war, politics, the pandemic, death, and so on, it doesn't make them negative people. These are just topics of conversation.

The problem arises when they add a toxic positivity spin to the conversation.

A good idea is to create anti-toxic positivity buddies. You can even have a modified swear jar into which everyone pays when they use a toxic positive phrase. Because it is so common, having a buddy system to monitor toxic positivity will help break the habit. You will also find that it becomes easier to talk about these difficult emotions that both of you would have otherwise suppressed.

Put it into practice

Our final practice is to write a letter to your past self. Remember that other people aren't aware of toxic positivity, just as you may not have been before reading this book. To help others better understand, practice writing to your past self and explain what you have learned and how you have benefited.

Include what toxic positivity means to you and some of the phrases you have used. Talk about your emotions and how you can now manage them by using specific techniques. Tell your old self how free you feel now that toxic positivity isn't weighing you down.

CONCLUSION

Positivity and a positive mindset are both wonderful and amazing things. They lead us to enjoy the present. As a result, we are more empathetic and creative, and our mental and physical health improves.

Positivity isn't toxic until it is forced upon us.

As soon as people or society start telling us that we should feel happy, we begin to question who we are. Negative self-talk, guilt for these feelings, and shame can cause anxiety and depression and potential health problems.

For those who have suffered from years of negativity and overthinking, it's easy to fall into the trap of repeating a few affirmations and expecting life to be positive. As if all of a sudden, the glass will be half full.

Only when we can be realistic about positivity will we see the benefits. And the reality is, life is hard.

> *"To deny that life has its share of disappointments, frustrations, losses, hurts, setbacks, and sadness would be unrealistic and untenable. Life is suffering. No amount of positive thinking exercises will change this truth."*
>
> — ROBERT EMMONS

Emmons sums it up perfectly. It is unrealistic to live in a world full of unicorns and rainbows. If it's not a pandemic, something else will trigger pain and suffering. No amount of positive vibes and energy is going to stop this.

The fact is, many people still can't see this as realism but as negativity. For them, it's better to ignore all the bad and pretend it doesn't exist. They are yet to see that this limits their life experiences.

Our emotions are incredibly complex, and when we start to understand that each emotion has a purpose, it is obvious why emotions shouldn't be suppressed.

Every emotion is valid. It's rather arrogant to tell someone to be grateful when we don't understand their pain. It's ignorant to say that life will get better when no one knows what lies ahead.

Rather than listening to toxic positivity and questioning the type of person you are, use the techniques in this book to better understand who you are, why you have these thoughts and emotions, and how to deal with them.

If I had to choose three techniques to help you develop a healthy way of thinking today, I would say mindfulness, goals, and journaling. These techniques don't require heavy analysis or any form of financial investment. All you need is time.

Scientists and even skeptics have proved that mindfulness has numerous mental and physical health benefits. For example, mindfulness can help us remain centered and find inner calm in times of great stress and worry.

You can use the RAIN method or guided meditation videos to help get you started. Remember, it's best to start with just a few minutes at a time and set aside time for two or three sessions a day. The benefits of mindfulness begin to decrease after twenty minutes, so it's not a case that the longer you do it, the more positive you become.

Goals keep us focused, driven, and disciplined. Goals are not only related to the bigger things in life. For example, most of us will want to pay off our mortgage or take that holiday we have always wanted. Don't forget that to reach long-term goals, start with short-term goals to keep the motivation going.

Finally, journaling has helped me extraordinarily. As someone who was constantly told that I should feel this or I shouldn't talk about that, I was very reluctant to speak to anyone about what my life was really like.

Writing in a journal allows you to practice talking about your emotions without fearing judgment. It also gives you time to work through the challenges you face in life and the complex emotions that come with them.

Learning how to overcome toxic positivity and develop a more optimistic outlook requires patience and dedication. So first, choose a few that connect with you from all of the strategies you have learned. Then, commit to working on these techniques every day for at least six weeks so that they become a natural part of your routine.

Even then, you will still have obstacles and difficult people to deal with. Be proud of how you manage your emotions. While you aren't responsible for other people's behavior or emotions, you can choose how you respond to them.

Don't get angry with those who still spout toxic positivity. We can all hold our hands up and admit that we have been guilty of it. Nevertheless, now that you know exactly how to overcome this forced, fake mentality, you are ready to avoid toxic positivity and gradually help others see the dangers.

On that note, I would be so grateful if you could leave a quick review on Amazon. This way, others can benefit in the same way you have, and together, we can create a more realistic vision of positivity. Thank you and good luck–I have complete faith in you.

SOME BOOKS YOU MAY FIND INTERESTING

How to Stop Negative Thinking

The 7-Step Plan to Eliminate Negativity, Overcome Rumination, Cease Overthinking Spiral, and Change Your Toxic Thoughts to Healthy Self-Talk

Are you fed up with people telling you to JUST be more positive?

Negative thinking isn't as simple as someone looking at the glass half empty. It is a **debilitating mindset** that seeps into every area of your life.

It can cause you to freeze in fear, withdraw from the world, and lose your relationships.

The constant rumination that keeps you up at night

spirals out of control. Your past mistakes keep replaying in your head, so much so this past version of yourself is all you can see.

Negative thinking happens automatically – **it's not your fault.**

Our brains thrive on negativity. Research published in *Psychological Bulletin* (2008) has proved that our brains are wired to think negatively.

You tell yourself that today will be a better day, but your brain tells you the opposite, and you slip back into old negative habits.

But that doesn't mean that negative thinking is something you can't control.

The brain is indeed negatively biased. However, science has confirmed that **you can rewire the way you think**. And you can start doing this today!

In *How to Stop Negative Thinking*, here is just a fraction of what you will discover:

• How to **overcome every type of negative thinking** from intrusive thoughts to rumination in 7 simple steps

• Simple, effective strategies with **practice exercises** that will help you overcome the negative thought patterns that prevent you from leading the life you want

- 3 crucial tools you can use to pinpoint the roots of your negative thinking

- **Scientifically proven breathing techniques** that will ease the impact of negative thoughts and rumination

- How to **put a stop to toxic behavior, passive aggression, and toxic positivity** and protect your new mindset

- **How to love and accept yourself despite your negative thinking** -- discover why this is crucial to kickstart your journey towards a happier, more positive person

And much more.

I know you have tried to stop your negative thinking, and nothing has worked. And the last thing you need is someone else telling you it's your attitude.

Your inner critic will be telling you that you can't do this or that you don't deserve to be happy. As soon as you understand how your brain works, that inner critic won't have a leg to stand on! You will have a clean slate to start this incredible journey towards positivity.

Just by reading this, you have taken control and decided to change. Now all that's missing is the final step.

**If you are ready to take the next step towards a

more positive life, then scan the QR code right now.

Healthy Boundaries

How to Set Strong Boundaries, Say No Without Guilt, and Maintain Good Relationships With Your Parents, Family, and Friends

Discover the power of self-love, and learn how to set healthy boundaries -- without feeling guilty.

Do you ever wonder what it would be like if the people you care about respected your personal space?

Do you wish that there was an easy way to say "No" every time you don't want to say "Yes"?

Or do you simply want to pursue self-love and not feel guilty about it?

If this is you, then you've probably had moments of trying to please others -- often, to your own detriment.

Perhaps you have an inability to say "No" because you don't want to disappoint or anger the other person… leading you to do things you never wanted to do in the first place…

If this happens too often, eventually, people will start taking you for granted -- and you won't be taken seriously even when you try to say "No."

What's worse, when you do try to set up boundaries, people will label you as mean or moody. It will seem impossible to make people respect your decisions without starting conflict.

But there's a simple way to solve your problems!

You can start doing what YOU want to do.

You don't have to compromise your individuality just to be "considerate" of others.

You can set healthy boundaries, and make your friends, family and parents **respect that boundary.**

In *Healthy Boundaries*, here's just a taste of what you'll discover:

• **A step-by-step guide to setting healthy personal boundaries without starting an argument**

• 5 dangerous mistakes you *must* avoid when setting boundaries

• The secret to saying "No" **without feeling guilty** -- and without being misunderstood

• How to stop constantly apologizing, and find out when you should and shouldn't be sorry

• 10 debilitating myths that are stopping you from setting up boundaries -- and how to troubleshoot them

• How to detoxify your emotions and release toxicity from your system like a breath of fresh air

• **A clear path to give you the freedom to love yourself, follow what YOU want, and prioritize yourself**

And *much more.*

Setting up boundaries isn't about being rude: it's about acknowledging that **your well-being comes first.** When you feel good, everything around you will be affected positively -- including the people you care about.

You don't have to shield everyone else from pain anymore -- realize that you're the one who's hurting, and do something about it. If you're ready to start living the life you deserve without feeling guilty, then scan the QR code below now!

Toxic People Survival Guide

How to Deal with Difficult, Negative, or Manipulative People, Handle Narcissists and Disarm Sociopaths

Break free from the toxic people in your life – the negativity and manipulation stop here! This is how you build the life you deserve:

Do you feel like you're constantly walking on eggshells trying to keep the peace, worried that your next action might cause that toxic friend or family member to explode... again?

Are you constantly questioning what's real and what's not, feeling confused and lost in a life that used to feel so much better?

Maybe you're wondering where the time has gone and how you've managed to drift so far from your goals and personal aspirations?

It's not uncommon to drift a bit from your path, but if you feel like it's been this way for far too long, then chances are it's not actually your fault.

If your life seems surrounded by negativity and limiting beliefs that don't align with who you are, you're not alone.

It's normal to sometimes be stuck with situations and people you don't want to deal with, but when these occurrences begin to negatively affect your own wellbeing, then it's time to do something about it.

No matter where you're at in life, how much experience you have dealing with difficult people, or how long you've felt adrift – ***you can break free!***

You don't have to continue to deal with the negativity just because those who create it in your life have been with you for so long.

Whether it's your boss, your partner, or even your closest friends and family, you can tell them 'no' and empower yourself into a whole new way of living – free from their control and influence.

With these **practical and effective tools and daily practices**, you'll soon find that the life you've always dreamt of living is a lot closer than you think.

In *Toxic People*, you'll discover:

• **How to spot toxic behavior** before it takes hold of your life, empowering you towards a calmer and more serene life

• Why there will always be difficult and sometimes toxic people in your life – and what you can do to navigate these situations with ease

• What your beliefs say about the world you allow around you – and how you can address and change these into something more desirable

• Why all toxic people aren't necessarily doomed – and the key things you can do to help both yourself and this person (especially if you really care about them)

• How to deal with the toxic people you can't remove

from your life by setting healthy boundaries and sticking to them

• **7 of the most powerful tactics you can use today** to overcome the manipulation of others

• Effective tips and tricks for you to enhance your daily life and begin building a more emotionally stable lifestyle for yourself

… and *much more!*

There's no need to sacrifice a ton of your time, money, or energy.

The manipulation and control stop here.

It stops today!

It's up to you to take back control of your life and get rid of all the things that are weighing you down.

If you're ready to move forward into a life of joy and peace, then scan the QR code below to order this book from Amazon page:

How to Stop Overthinking

The 7-Step Plan to Control and Eliminate Negative Thoughts, Declutter Your Mind and Start Thinking Positively in 5 Minutes or Less

Do you find yourself lying awake at night because you can't stop worrying about what happened today? Are you constantly second-guessing almost every decision that you are faced with in life? Do your job, friendships or whole life seem to be overwhelming?

By reading this book, you will emboldened yourself to deal with your fears, anxiety, handle your perfectionism, and stop your overthinking for good.

What you should expect along the journey of practicing the techniques and strategies throughout this book is to be aware of where your mental chatter comes from, and how to address it.

Stop worrying about what you did today and start living in the moment. Stop living for tomorrow and start breathing in the positivity of today. Stop overthinking your future and make big changes to live your future now.

We are only ever promised today, so instead of obsessing over what you could have done at that social event or trying to control what you will do in your next appointment, learn to breathe in this moment you have now.

What you'll learn:

• How to Control Overthinking and Eliminate Negative Thoughts in Just a Few Minutes.

• 10 Powerful Tactics to Stop Anxiety and Worrying Permanently.

• How to Sleep Better, Even if Your Head Is Full of Thoughts.

• Simple Tips to Develop Self-Confidence and Decision-Making Skills.

• How to Remove Toxicity and Change Your Relationships for the Better.

• 5 Ways to Calm Anxiety (Worrying) in Five Minutes or Less.

• Troubleshooting Guide if Nothing Helps.

• How to Declutter Your Mind and Become What You Want in Life.

This book will go through the reasons why the way you think now is not beneficial to your being and how positivity can greatly improve your outlook and put yourself in the direction you want your life to go.

So, quit being stuck, stop letting your mind trap you, and take control of what you want. There are finally lessons and a structure to get you to where you **want** to be rather than where you are now. AND, it's all in this book.

Would You Like To Know More?

Grab this book to get started and turn off your overthinking for good!

Scan the QR code below to order it from Amazon immediately.

* * *

Stop People Pleasing

How to Start Saying No, Set Healthy Boundaries, and Express Yourself

Do you say yes to people so often, you've forgotten how it feels to say no?

You're not alone.

Many people spend years putting aside their own wants and needs in order to please the people in their life and avoid conflict. Although there will always be situations where diplomacy is important, **you cannot define your life through other people**.

There's a fine line between being considerate of others, and compromising your individuality, and you can slip into living as a people-pleaser without even realizing it.

Maybe you've been going through the routines of life

feeling that you must keep quiet, and take responsibility for the feelings of others.

Or, maybe you think it's more important to avoid "rocking the boat" than it is to be **your most authentic self**.

While these habits might seem to dominate everything you do, there are actionable steps you can take to create a new world--one where you are open and confident in what you say and do.

Just like the relationships you have with others, everyone's experiences with people-pleasing are unique. However, this individuality often stems from common roots that are keeping you trapped in the box of others' expectations.

By helping you identify the steps that will assist you the most, Chase Hill shows it is possible to start changing, right here and right now.

In *Stop People Pleasing*, you will discover:

• The **10 signs** that indicate people-pleasing characteristics, besides the inability to say no

• A step-by-step **14-day action plan** to help you achieve instant and notable improvements

• The **4 defense mechanisms specific to people pleasing**, how to identify them, and how to respond to them

• Multiple exercises and approaches to help you

rediscover who you are at heart, breaking free from feeling the need to seek validation from others

• Coping mechanisms designed to help you overcome discomfort or frustration as you redefine the boundaries in your life

If you believe it's impossible to finally stand up to your in-laws or be honest with your friends, think again.

You deserve to **make the choices that YOU want to make**, and speak your mind without fear or anxiety.

There's no quick fix for people-pleasing. Like most important things, changing your patterns will take time.

With the right tools and techniques by your side, you will be able to hit the ground running and be one step closer to living your life the way *you* want to live it.

If you're ready to finally stand up for yourself and transform your life, scan the QR code below to order this book from Amazon page!

YOUR FREE EBOOK

29 WAYS TO OVERCOME NEGATIVE THOUGHTS

I'd like to give you a gift as a way of saying thanks for your purchase!

* * *

In 29 Ways to Overcome Negative Thoughts, you'll discover:

- 10 Strategies to Reduce Negativity in Your Life
- 7 Steps to Quickly Stop Negative Thoughts
- 12 Powerful Tips to Beat Negative Thinking

To receive your Free Ebook, visit the link:

free.chasehillbooks.com

Alternatively, you can scan the QR-code below:

If you have any difficulty downloading the ebook, contact me at chase@chasehillbooks.com, and I'll send you a copy as soon as possible.

RESOURCES

Adler, J. M. (2012, April 23). Mixed Emotional Experience Is Associated with and Precedes Improvements in Psychological Well-Being. Journals Plos. Retrieved November 15, 2021, from https://journals.plos.org/plosone/article?id=10.1371/journal.pone.0035633

American Psychiatric Association. (n.d.). Stigma and Discrimination against People with Mental Illness. Psychiatry Org. Retrieved November 15, 2021, from https://www.psychiatry.org/patients-families/stigma-and-discrimination

Ayala, E. E. (2018, August 6). U.S. medical students who engage in self-care report less stress and higher quality of life. NCBI NLM NIH. Retrieved November 15, 2021, from https://www.ncbi.nlm.nih.gov/pmc/articles/PMC6080382/

Baer, D. (2016, June 14). How Only Being Able to Use Logic to Make Decisions Destroyed a Man's Life. The Cut. Retrieved

November 15, 2021, from https://www.thecut.com/2016/06/how-only-using-logic-destroyed-a-man.html

Burchell, B. H. (2021, February 2). Capt Sir Tom Moore: How the retired Army officer became a nation's hero. BBC News. Retrieved November 15, 2021, from https://www.bbc.com/news/uk-england-beds-bucks-herts-52324058

C. (2020, September 22). Most Common Things That People Overthink! 107.5 Kool FM. Retrieved November 15, 2021, from https://1075koolfm.com/most-common-things-that-people-overthink/

Casabianca, S. S. (2021, May 6). Stuck in the Negatives? 15 Cognitive Distortions To Blame. Psych Central. Retrieved November 15, 2021, from https://psychcentral.com/lib/cognitive-distortions-negative-thinking#types

Children's National. (n.d.). Children's National Hospital - Ranked #1 for Newborn Care and One of the Top 10 Best Children's Hospitals in the Nation. Childrensnational. Retrieved November 15, 2021, from https://childrensnational.org

Chowdhury, M. R. (2021a, September 13). How to Foster Compassion at Work Through Compassionate Leadership. PositivePsychology.Com. Retrieved November 15, 2021, from https://positivepsychology.com/compassion-at-work-leadership/

Chowdhury, M. R. (2021b, September 13). How to Foster Compassion at Work Through Compassionate Leadership. PositivePsychology.Com. Retrieved November 15, 2021, from https://positivepsychology.com/compassion-at-work-leadership/

Contributors to Wikimedia projects. (2021, November 10). *Does objective reality exist?* Wikiversity. Retrieved November 15, 2021, from https://en.wikiversity.org/wiki/Does_objective_reality_exist%3F

Cornerstone. (n.d.). *10 Companies Putting Empathy into Action.* Conerstone Demand. Retrieved November 15, 2021, from https://www.cornerstoneondemand.com/resources/blogs/10-companies-putting-empathy-action/

D'Angelo, S. (2020, November 6). *Research Paper: The Importance of Self-Care.* International Coach Academy. Retrieved November 15, 2021, from https://coachcampus.com/coach-portfolios/research-papers/sandra-dangelo-the-importance-of-self-care/

DoctorRamani. (2020, October 9). *When narcissists use positivity to control you* [Video]. YouTube. https://www.youtube.com/watch?v=bWH1iRSIzxs

Ellard, K. K., Barlow, D. H., Whitfield-Gabrieli, S., Gabrieli, J. D. E., & Deckersbach, T. (2017, April 11). *Neural correlates of emotion acceptance vs worry or suppression in generalized anxiety disorder.* OUP Academic. Retrieved November 15, 2021, from https://academic.oup.com/scan/article/12/6/1009/3574843

Forgas, J. P. (2014, June 4). *Four Ways Sadness May Be Good for You.* Greater Good. Retrieved November 15, 2021, from https://greatergood.berkeley.edu/article/item/four_ways_sadness_may_be_good_for_you

Fredrickson, B. L., & Cohn, M. A. (2011, August 15). *Open*

Hearts Build Lives: Positive Emotions, Induced Through Loving-Kindness Meditation, Build Consequential Personal Resources. NCBI NLM NIH. Retrieved November 15, 2021, from https://www.ncbi.nlm.nih.gov/pmc/articles/PMC3156028/

Garone, S. (2020, February 25). Mood Journal 101: How to Get Started on Controlling Your Emotions. Healthline. Retrieved November 15, 2021, from https://www.healthline.com/health/how-to-keep-mood-journal#How-to-keep-a-mood-journal

Goldman, B. (2015, May 28). Researchers tie unexpected brain structures to creativity— and to stifling it. Med. Stanford. Retrieved November 15, 2021, from https://med.stanford.edu/news/all-news/2015/05/researchers-tie-unexpected-brain-structures-to-creativity.html

Grossman, I., Huynh, A. C., & Ellsworth, P. C. (2016). Emotional Complexity: Clarifying definitions and cultural correlates. Psycnet.Apa. Retrieved November 15, 2021, from https://psycnet.apa.org/record/2015-57060-001

How to Use the RAIN Method for Difficult Emotions | GRW Health Blog. (2019, April 3). GRW Health. Retrieved November 15, 2021, from https://www.grwhealth.com/post/how-to-use-the-rain-method-for-difficult-emotions

Hurley, T. (2020a, January 3). Activating the Parasympathetic Nervous System to Decrease Stress and Anxiety. Canyon Vista Recovery Center. Retrieved November 15, 2021, from https://canyonvista.com/activating-parasympathetic-nervous-system/

Hurley, T. (2020b, January 3). Activating the Parasympathetic

Nervous System to Decrease Stress and Anxiety. *Canyon Vista Recovery Center.* Retrieved November 15, 2021, from https://canyonvista.com/activating-parasympathetic-nervous-system/

In The Know. (2020, September 19). *What is toxic positivity — and why it's a big problem during the pandemic* [Video]. YouTube. https://www.youtube.com/watch?v=91Yfy0QCHic

Institute for Social Research University of Michigan. (n.d.). *Bittersweet symphony: Researchers try to untangle mixed emotions. Institute for Social Research.* Retrieved November 15, 2021, from https://isr.umich.edu/news-events/insights-newsletter/article/bittersweet-symphony-researchers-try-untangle-mixed-emotions/

Jabra. (2021). *Jabra Hybrid Ways of Working: 2021 Global Report.* Retrieved November 15, 2021, from https://www.jabra.es/hybridwork

Karimova, H., MA. (2021, May 20). *The Emotion Wheel: What It Is and How to Use It [+PDF]. PositivePsychology.Com.* Retrieved November 15, 2021, from https://positivepsychology.com/emotion-wheel/

Kaufman, S. B. (2021, August 18). *Tragic Optimism Is the Opposite of Toxic Positivity. The Atlantic.* Retrieved November 15, 2021, from https://www.theatlantic.com/family/archive/2021/08/tragic-optimism-opposite-toxic-positivity/619786/

Kleppinger, U. (2021, March 11). *The Cult of Oppressive Positivity. PREGAME.* Retrieved November 15, 2021, from https://pregamehq.com/cult-oppressive-positivity/

Kross, E. (2014). *Self-talk as a regulatory mechanism: How you* do it matters. DOI APA. Retrieved November 15, 2021, from https://doi.apa.org/doiLanding?doi=10.1037%2Fa0035173

Krpan, K. (2013, September 25). An everyday activity as a treatment for depression: The benefits of expressive writing for people diagnosed with major depressive disorder. ScienceDirect. Retrieved November 15, 2021, from https://www.sciencedirect.com/science/article/abs/pii/S0165032713004448

Kuppens, B. B. (2012). Feeling bad about being sad: The role of social expectancies in amplifying negative mood.Psycnet.Org. Retrieved November 15, 2021, from https://psycnet.apa.org/record/2011-15463-001

Lawler, M., & Laube, J., MD. (2021, May 19). What Is Self-Care and Why Is It Critical for Your Health? EverydayHealth.Com. Retrieved November 15, 2021, from https://www.everydayhealth.com/self-care/

Long, J. (2021, March 13). Toxic Positivity: The Dark Side of Positive Vibes. The Psychology Group Fort Lauderdale. Retrieved November 15, 2021, from https://thepsychologygroup.com/toxic-positivity/

Most women think too much, overthinkers often drink too much - UM News Service. (2003, February 4). Ns.Umich. Retrieved November 15, 2021, from http://ns.umich.edu/Releases/2003/Feb03/r020403c.html

NeuroFocus Physiotherapy & Sports Injury Clinic. (2017, July 28). Using desks with a standing capability may increase work productivity. Retrieved November 15, 2021, from https://neurofocusphysio.ca/library_newsfeed_841/

Ozaki, K. (2012, April 1). Association between psychological distress and a sense of contribution to society in the workplace. BMC Public Health. Retrieved November 15, 2021, from https://bmcpublichealth.biomedcentral.com/articles/10.1186/1471-2458-12-253

Patel, J., & Patel, P. (2019, February 12). Consequences of Repression of Emotion: Physical Health, Mental Health and General Well Being | Open Access Pub. Openaccesspub. Retrieved November 15, 2021, from https://openaccesspub.org/ijpr/article/999#ridm1850254004

Plutchik, R. (2001). The Nature of Emotions: Human emotions have deep evolutionary roots, a fact that may explain their complexity and provide tools for clinical practice. Jstor. Retrieved November 15, 2021, from https://www.jstor.org/stable/27857503?seq=1

Radin, S. (2021, August 4). How 'toxic positivity' took over the internet. Dazed. Retrieved November 15, 2021, from https://www.dazeddigital.com/life-culture/article/53737/1/how-toxic-positivity-took-over-the-internet

Robson, D. (2021, February 4). How too much mindfulness can spike anxiety. BBC Worklife. Retrieved November 15, 2021, from https://www.bbc.com/worklife/article/20210202-how-mindfulness-can-blunt-your-feelings-and-spike-anxiety

Schnall, S., Jaswal, V. K., & Rowe, C. (2008, October). A

hidden cost of happiness in children. Researchgate. Retrieved November 15, 2021, from https://www.researchgate.net/publication/23275883_A_hidden_cost_of_happiness_in_children

Scully, S. M. (2020, July 22). 'Toxic Positivity' Is Real — and It's a Big Problem During the Pandemic. Healthline. Retrieved November 15, 2021, from https://www.healthline.com/health/mental-health/toxic-positivity-during-the-pandemic#What-is-toxic-positivity

Sinclair, E., Hart, R., & Lomas, T. (2020). Can positivity be counterproductive when suffering domestic abuse?: A narrative review. Repository.Uel. Retrieved November 15, 2021, from https://repository.uel.ac.uk/item/8842y

Wagner, D. (2021, August 25). Polyvagal theory in practice. Counseling Today. Retrieved November 15, 2021, from https://ct.counseling.org/2016/06/polyvagal-theory-practice/

Wegner, D. M. (1987, July). Paradoxical effects of thought suppression. NIH. Retrieved November 15, 2021, from https://pubmed.ncbi.nlm.nih.gov/3612492/

World Health Organization. (2019, May 15). What do we mean by self-care? Retrieved November 15, 2021, from https://www.who.int/reproductivehealth/self-care-interventions/definitions/en/

Zak, H. (2021, January 5). Adults Make More Than 35,000 Decisions Per Day. Here Are 4 Ways to Prevent Mental Burnout. Inc.Com. Retrieved November 15, 2021, from https://www.inc.com/heidi-zak/adults-make-more-than-35000-decisions-per-day-here-are-4-ways-to-prevent-mental-burnout.html

Printed in Great Britain
by Amazon

813c84ca-139a-4f96-a017-7c561a23e10aR01